The Riversong
Lodge Cookbook

The Riversong Lodge Cookbook

World-Class Cooking in the Alaskan Bush

Kirsten Dixon

Alaska Northwest Books™
Anchorage • Seattle • Portland

Second printing 1994

Library of Congress Cataloging-in-Publication Data
Dixon, Kirsten
    The Riversong Lodge cookbook : world-class cooking in the
Alaskan bush / Kirsten Dixon.
       p.   cm.
    Includes bibliographical references and index.
    ISBN 0-88240-431-8
    ISBN 0-88240-397-4 (paper)
    1. Cookery, International. 2. Cookery—Alaska. 3. Riversong
Lodge. I. Title.
    TX725.A1D55 1993
    641.59—dc20   93-17711
                                          CIP

Managing Editor: Ellen Harkins Wheat
Editor: Rebecca Pepper
Designer: Cameron Mason
Illustrator: Debbie Hanley

Alaska Northwest Books™
An imprint of Graphic Arts Center Publishing Company
Editorial office: 2208 NW Market Street, Suite 300, Seattle, WA 98107
Catalog and order dept.: P.O. Box 10306, Portland, OR 97210
    800-452-3032

Printed on recycled paper in the United States of America

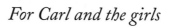

For Carl and the girls

Contents

Winter

Spring

Summer

Acknowledgments

My husband Carl built my kitchen with his own hands. He peeled the bark off the tree that became the room's center beam and he hauled my stoves up from the riverbank when they arrived by floatplane. Carl took care of our family while I went away to school. Thank you, Carl, for your love and friendship.

And for my daughters Carly and Amanda, when you are grown, I hope you never forget the delight you took as children in cooking breakfasts with your dad. Big, fluffy pancakes in the shape of C for Carly and M for Manda are your current specialties. Thanks for being such great kids.

I cannot recall how many glasses of water I knocked over onto my mother's plate just after the entrée had been served when I was a child. Nevertheless, my parents, James and Peggy Schmidt, undauntedly took me along with them to wonderful tables around the world and exposed me to treasured experiences with food. For that and so much more, I am grateful.

For my sisters, Katherine de Hoop and Jami Schmidt, I appreciate all the help along the way.

I would like to express my gratitude to Linda Sievers, food editor for the *Anchorage Daily News,* who encouraged me to write. From the lodge, I have sent articles to her by nearly every conceivable mode of transportation—floatplane, skiplane, or snow machine—and she has never complained about the shape they're in when they arrive. I have appreciated our friendship.

I admire Anne Willan tremendously for her hard work and pursuit of perfection. She inspires me to do more. Jacques Pépin is a generous teacher and encourages me to continue in my academic growth.

Thank you to the authors who have allowed me to include their recipes in this collection. A special thanks to Carl Sontheimer, for sending me cookbooks and for the use of the Homemade Marshmallow recipe (copyright 1984), Anne Willan for the use of her recipes for Salmon in Brioche Crust (copyright 1985) and Quick Brioche Dough (copyright 1985), and Margaret Leibenstein for allowing me to adapt her Morels Stuffed with Shrimp Mousse recipe.

At Alaska Northwest Books, Marlene Blessing, Ellen Wheat, and Rebecca Pepper are the greatest!

And a special thanks to my friend Robert Warren for teaching me about wines.

The Riversong Lodge Cookbook

The Riversong Lodge Region

The Riversong Lodge Kitchen

No roads lead to the Riversong Lodge kitchen. The kitchen is built on the back side of our log house, which sits on the bank of a river in rural Alaska. The kitchen windows are lined with lace curtains and look out over the herb garden and beyond to the surrounding wild woods of spruce, alder, and birch. Large black stoves command one wall and a solid hardwood work table fills the center of the room. The pantry shelves are stocked with our preserved harvest, and the root cellar houses wines and cheeses. From this kitchen come the foods that we lovingly prepare for our Riversong guests—and share with you in this collection.

I arrived in Alaska in 1980, young and just out of nursing school. I had received a scholarship to Syracuse University from the U.S. Public Health Service, and in return I worked at the Alaska Native Medical Center for two years. The first person I met in Anchorage was Carl, my future husband. Carl was working at the medical center as an audiologist. He had been in Anchorage since 1974, originally coming to Alaska on a temporary job assignment with the state of Alaska and with no intention of staying. Needless to say, he never left.

When I met Carl, he was preparing to leave his job at the hospital and start an outdoor river-rafting company. He made the break in March 1981, and began to explore Alaska's rivers and backcountry full time.

We were married December 13, 1981. I was 24 years old and he was 31. A year later, our first daughter, Carly, was born. Our interests centered around home and family, yet we had little time to be together. I was working nights in the intensive care unit at the hospital and Carl was traveling extensively. Carly was spending her days and sometimes nights with people we hardly knew. We began to look for some way to change our lives.

Carl had been taking guests on float fishing trips for a few years before I met him, at first privately with friends and then commercially to help pay his way to remote places. It was on such a float trip during the summer of 1983, down a river called Lake Creek, that he saw the property we now call Riversong. He made inquiries, found out it was for sale, bought it in July, and we moved there in September.

Riversong overlooks the banks of the Yentna River, which runs from west to east, 70 miles northwest of Anchorage. Lake Creek flows into the Yentna River near the lodge. The area in a ten-mile radius from the lodge is known as Lake Creek. Before we moved to Riversong, I had never seen Lake Creek, or very much of Alaska outside of Anchorage for that matter. With one small child, another baby to be born soon, little money, no experience in wilderness living, and no knowledge about the business of running a lodge, we set out to start our new life.

The next few years seemed to rush by. The hard work was over-whelming at times. Everything happened at once—small children to look after, a lodge to build, guests to care for, and animals and a garden to tend. We worked hard, determined never to let the odds discourage us. For Carl and me, Riversong has become a rich and unique place, filled with enough good work for us for a lifetime. Here, every day is different, and every day the importance of living close to the earth is revealed to us.

When I think back, I had always liked to cook. The interest was there, tucked away in my consciousness, but I never considered turning cooking into a profession. I started by helping Carl prepare the food for some of his first river trips, making jumbo batches of cookies and sweet breads. I discovered cooking magazines and books, and began teaching myself how to make different dishes. When we moved to Lake Creek, I enthusiastically embraced the challenge of being the lodge cook.

In the beginning, we had our stove behind the bar in our one-room lodge. I hung our pots and pans from the log beams overhead. The first year we operated Riversong, 1984, we had one guest cabin that could accommodate four guests. I cooked on our small stove and would talk with guests as they watched me work. While I served dinner, Carly sat in a high chair on the back porch and Amanda dozed in a bassinet covered with mosquito netting.

Two years after we opened the lodge, we built a small kitchen where the back porch had been. I still had a regular-sized stove, and the kitchen was small but efficiently laid out. I served meals family-style, using lots of casserole dishes and big platters. Bread baking was the biggest task. At first, to generate some extra business, I made hamburgers and chili for people who might stop in off the river, so every three days, I would make a large batch of hamburger buns and freeze them. In later years, we became too busy with our own guests to offer à la carte meals to people just dropping in.

Eventually, we decided to hire someone to help us with the girls. Shortly thereafter, Carl brought in another fishing guide. We added a staff person here and there, a new cabin, another boat and motor. We soon began to feel cramped in our one-room lodge. The next addition, after the small kitchen, was a glass greenhouse. I had entered a contest being held by *Self* magazine called "Fresh Start," which awarded grants to women who wanted to do something to change their lives. My desire was to build a glass greenhouse adjoining the lodge, where I could grow herb and vegetable seedlings to put into the garden in early summer. Much to my delight, I won the contest and was given a $7,500 grant to build our new room. When the greenhouse was completed, Carl used a chain saw to cut a doorway through the log wall between the greenhouse and the east side of the lodge. I was terrified to see him cut into the logs, but when he had finished, light flooded into the lodge. The greenhouse has been one of our most used rooms ever since.

Next came the dining room. Built on the west side of the lodge, it displays one of our prized possessions—an upright piano we brought by boat all the way from Anchorage. Two large tables that each seat ten people occupy the center of the room. The floor is planked wood covered with blue Oriental carpets. After the dining room we built the new kitchen where we now work. The old kitchen is next to it, and serves as a dishwashing room and a dining room for the staff.

We now have nine guest cabins that can sleep up to 35 guests, and a staff of 18 employees. I have three chefs in the kitchen to help me, and Carl has ten fishing guides. We are a bigger and better lodge than we ever dreamed we would be. We serve three big meals a day, plus staff meals. Guests eat in the dining room, the main room, and the greenhouse when the lodge is full. All of our food is fresh, all breads are baked daily, and we make our own desserts. It's a hard-working group in the kitchen. In the fall, our guests and employees leave, and Carl and I return to the quieter life that we originally sought at Lake Creek.

We now serve meals on individual plates rather than family style. Breakfasts are hearty, big affairs to start a day of fishing off right. Lunch is a hot soup, salad, pasta or sandwiches, and always a large platter of cookies. At dinner, we serve a first course, an entrée, and a dessert. Some people make reservations and fly out to Riversong from Anchorage just to have meals with us.

Once a week, the kitchen staff and I sit down to plan the menus. We take into consideration the tastes of the various guests staying at the lodge at the time—often from different parts of the globe.

Certain childhood experiences with food have been strong influences in my approach to cooking. I remember especially my grandmother, Asta Schmidt, a spirited Californian transplant from Denmark, who was a great cook. I knew that she was a good cook long before I knew what good cooking was. I heard people talk about her food when she wasn't around. I sensed the pleasure of the adults around me when they ate a meal she had prepared.

I recall the tastes and smells from one occasion vividly. We were sitting at her kitchen table in the summer. The room was bright and breezy, with a back screen door that opened onto a green and shady yard. Asta went out and plucked a few plump, ripe peaches from a tree. She carefully peeled and sliced the biggest peach into a bowl and placed it in front of me. From a small ceramic pitcher, she poured just enough cold heavy cream to coat the slices of fragrant peach.

"Mmm, that is a perfect peach. Do you taste the sweetness?" she said. I embraced my bowl, pleased that I was important enough to be served something so perfect. When my bowl was empty, my grandmother shooed me out the door. The smell of lilacs and fruit trees mingled with the warmth of the sun, and I felt happy and energetic.

Looking back on that vivid memory, I realize how important food is to our emotional well-being. Good food doesn't have to be complex or expensive. In fact, the simplest of fresh, nutritious foods can often bring the greatest aesthetic pleasure. I learned this from my grandmother.

It takes caring and concern to be a good cook. It requires a certain commitment in life-style as well, a refusal to compromise on quality. In my first years at the lodge, I was often frustrated in my attempt to acquire the knowledge I needed to be a cook. Since then, my repertoire has expanded. I have attended classes at the Cordon Bleu school in Paris, I've studied culinary history with Jacques Pépin at Boston University, and I have collected and used many of the wonderful new cookbooks that are bringing knowledge into kitchens everywhere.

The recipes in this book are samples of the foods we prepare in our life at Riversong. Since there are many excellent "how-to" books that cover the basics, I haven't included recipes for such items as chicken stock and mayonnaise. Instead, I have chosen dishes that are distinctive samples from the Riversong kitchen. This cookbook also does not focus on low-cholesterol, low-fat cooking. Many of my recipes feature butter, eggs, and cream—country food for hard-working people.

The Riversong Lodge Cookbook is organized by season. Each chapter begins with a story about our lives at the lodge, followed by seasonal menus and recipes. The chapters also move through time from the first days at Riversong to the present, and if you look closely, you can see my cuisine changing through the years. Throughout, I've tried to keep my recipes easy to prepare.

Alaska has its own cuisine. Some foods that are plentiful here are nearly impossible to find anywhere else. Salmon, of course, is frequently on our menu, as are other Alaskan seafoods. We eat moose and caribou, and sometimes other game. We pick fresh flower petals to garnish the plates, wild berries for desserts, and greens from our bountiful garden for fresh salads. For foods that might not be readily available outside Alaska, I've provided a list of mail-order sources at the back of the book and indicated substitutes where appropriate.

A note on some ingredients in my recipes: I use unsalted butter in all the recipes in this book because unsalted butter can be fresher than salted, in terms of shelf life and flavor. I understand, however, that unsalted butter is not available for some rural people. In that case, simply substitute regular butter and adjust the salt to your taste. For game meats or wild berries that I use but that you might not have access to, try the recipe anyway, substituting favorite meats or fruits. I prefer canola oil for most recipes, but other oils can be substituted. Hot-smoked salmon is kippered salmon. The flavor of hot-smoked salmon varies with the smokehouse, but it is more intense and somewhat saltier than that of cold-smoked salmon, also known as lox. Hot-smoked salmon is flakier and drier than lox, which is fleshy and best sliced thin. I don't think hot-smoked salmon and cold-smoked salmon are inter-changeable in recipes—the textures and flavors of the fish are too different.

The Riversong Lodge Cookbook, I hope, will help you experience a bit of our lives and the wonderful foods we eat at the lodge. If you haven't been to Alaska, I urge you to come. I'll cook you a nice hot stew and we'll linger near the wood stove, telling tales of life along the river.

Winter

The First Day

The morning was gray with early winter. The mountains that rim Anchorage had been covered with snow for weeks. It was cold enough to make my breath freeze as I stood on the dock that extended out into Lake Hood, the world's largest floatplane base, located on the outskirts of Anchorage. Carly, our one-year-old daughter, was bundled in the pack on my back while I sorted through boxes and bags piled next to the floatplane. Her head bobbed from side to side as I bent down to examine the supplies we had spent weeks assembling. She peeked around my shoulder as if watching over my activities and pushed impatiently on the bottom bar of the pack with her fur-lined booties. Duncan, our black Labrador, sniffed and scurried along the wooden planks of the dock. Today we were moving to our new home on the Yentna River.

I had spent two weeks gathering provisions. I wasn't sure how much to buy or what items would be important as the winter moved on, so I made guesses: 100 pounds of All Montana hard wheat white flour, 50 pounds of whole wheat flour, 3 pounds of yeast, powdered eggs to supplement the 30 dozen fresh eggs, meats, fruits, diapers, dry goods, and candles. Tucked among the cabbages and blocks of butter were waterproof matches and treasured caches of books. I had packed a supper in case it was late when we settled in—ham, a few boiled potatoes, and a loaf of bread.

Finally the small plane was loaded. I sat in the backseat with Carly still strapped in her backpack. Duncan was at my feet, slobbering nervously onto my black rubber knee boots—called "breakup boots" here. My kitchen broom and floor mop straddled my lap. With a roar of its engines, the plane took to the air, gaining altitude as it soared past the rooftops of Anchorage and out over Cook Inlet, heading north toward the Upper Susitna Valley.

Forty minutes later, our pilot, Glen Curtis, circled above the location of what was to become Riversong Lodge and landed expertly on the Yentna River just as the sun was setting. Large, portentous snowflakes fell as we dodged early ice floes in the current.

Once we were safely ashore, we lumbered up the hill to the neglected one-room cabin that would be our home for the next year. The cabin was small and dark. Optimism filled us so completely that nothing could have daunted our spirit—not even the cabin's broken window or disheveled interior. Junk littered the yard: an old bedspring and a broken refrigerator lay against a small birch tree, bending it nearly to the ground. One of the first things Carl did was to free the tree of the carelessly placed burden and tie it up so that the little birch could grow straight.

Inside the cabin, we set about making things comfortable. A small propane stove, a table and two chairs, and a wood stove were our only furnishings. After searching for and finding those well-packed matches, we started a fire in the wood stove, lit the kerosene lamps that would be our only light source over the dark winter, and put Carly to sleep on a makeshift bed on the floor. As we savored our supper and toasted the day with a glass of wine by the flickering glow of our lantern, we listened to the silence of our new life on the river.

Wild Mushroom Barley Soup

At Riversong, we collect mushrooms in the spring. To preserve both wild and domestic mushrooms, we thread them onto long cotton strings and hang them near the wood stove to dry. This soup is robust and earthy and will bring warmth to the chilliest of days.

½ cup dried or fresh wild
  mushrooms (morels or
  oyster mushrooms)
1 cup barley
½ cup canola oil
1 large onion, peeled and
  finely chopped
2 large carrots, peeled and
  finely chopped
2 cloves garlic, peeled and
  minced
2 cups minced fresh domestic
  mushrooms
6 cups homemade or canned
  chicken stock
3 tablespoons lemon juice
Salt and freshly ground
  pepper to taste
2 cups heavy cream

If using dried wild mushrooms, soak them in hot water to cover for 30 minutes and drain. Bring 4 cups of water to a boil. Add the barley, cover, and simmer for 25 minutes over medium heat. Drain the barley and set aside.

Heat the oil in a large, heavy saucepan. Add the onion, carrots, and garlic, tossing to coat the vegetables in oil. Add the domestic mushrooms. Cover with aluminum foil, placing foil right on the surface of the vegetables. Simmer over low heat for 15 minutes.

Slice the wild mushrooms, leaving any small ones whole. Add the cooked barley, wild mushrooms, stock, and lemon juice to the pan. Season with salt and pepper to taste. Simmer for 10 minutes. Stir in the heavy cream and heat just to boiling. Serve immediately.

Makes 4 to 6 servings.

Cornish Pasties

Cornish pasties are small, meat-filled pies that were traditionally served to working men in the coal mines of England. When Carl was building the main lodge and wouldn't take a break, I'd make these portable pies, bundle up Carly, and we'd walk over for a visit. The pies also make good "river food" in the summer for fishermen who don't want to leave the water.

PASTY DOUGH:

Pastry for two 9-inch double-crust mealy pie shells (see "Two Kinds of Pie Crust" on pages 47 and 48)

FILLING:

3 tablespoons canola oil
1 clove garlic, peeled and minced
1 large onion, peeled and sliced into thin rings
1½ pounds flank steak, diced into ¼-inch cubes
2 medium baking potatoes, washed and diced into ¼-inch cubes (4 cups)
3 medium turnips, peeled and diced into ¼-inch cubes (4 cups)
Salt and freshly ground pepper to taste
3 tablespoons unsalted butter

Wrap the pastry dough in plastic wrap and chill until firm, 2 to 4 hours if possible.

To make the filling, heat the oil in a medium saucepan over medium heat. Add the garlic and sauté until the garlic is brown but not burned. Add the onion slices to the pan and coat well with the garlic and oil. Sauté the onions until they are golden in color. Remove the onion-garlic mixture from the pan and set aside. Return the pan to the heat and add the flank steak. Sear the meat over high heat, turning it frequently to brown all surfaces. Remove the flank steak from the pan. Combine the onion-garlic mixture, meat, potatoes, and turnips. Set aside.

Preheat the oven to 450 degrees Fahrenheit. Grease a baking sheet. Remove the dough from the refrigerator. Roll the dough out on a lightly floured surface to a thickness of approximately ⅛ inch. Cut 8-inch or smaller circles, using a plate or saucepan lid as a template and a sharp knife or a pastry cutter. Place the circles in the refrigerator until assembly time.

To assemble the pasties, place one pastry circle on a lightly floured surface. On one half of the dough, place enough of the beef mixture (about ½ cup) to fill, leaving a ½-inch edge around the pasty. Season with salt and pepper and add 1 teaspoon of the butter. Moisten the edge with a little cold water and fold over the pasty. Press the bottom and top edges together with your fingers, creating a scalloped effect. Place the pasty on the prepared baking sheet. Fill and fold the remaining pasties.

With a sharp knife, cut a small air vent in the top of each pasty. Place the baking sheet on the middle rack of the oven and reduce the heat to 400 degrees Fahrenheit. Bake for 15 minutes, reduce the heat to 325 degrees Fahrenheit, and continue baking for 30 minutes or until the pasties are golden brown. Serve hot.

Makes 8 to 12 servings.

Two-Potato Pie

We don't grow sweet potatoes in Alaska, but they store for long periods of time, so I always try to have them on hand in the root cellar. This pie can be served as an elegant side dish to accompany a rustic family meal, as a special-occasion dish, or even as a breakfast option. Serve in wedges with a dollop of sour cream or with Winter Cranberries (see page 38).

2 cloves garlic, peeled and mashed
2 tablespoons unsalted butter, at room temperature
1 pound large potatoes, peeled
1 pound sweet potatoes or yams, peeled
Salt and freshly ground pepper to taste
3 eggs, lightly beaten
2 cups heavy cream
1 teaspoon ground nutmeg

Preheat the oven to 450 degrees Fahrenheit. Blend the garlic and butter together and use to grease a 9-inch pie pan. Slice the potatoes and sweet potatoes paper-thin, either by hand or with a food processor. Place a layer of potatoes on the bottom of the pie pan. Sprinkle with salt and pepper to taste. Add a layer of sweet potatoes next. Sprinkle again with salt and pepper. Continue layering the potatoes. On the final layer, alternate potato and sweet potato slices to vary the color.

In a medium mixing bowl, whisk the eggs with the cream and nutmeg. Season to taste with salt and pepper. Pour the mixture over the potatoes slowly so that the custard doesn't run out before it is absorbed by the layers. Bake on the center rack of the oven for 30 minutes. Reduce the heat to 350 degrees Fahrenheit and bake 1 hour longer, or until the top is brown and the middle is firm. Serve in wedges.

Makes 4 to 6 servings.

Rules of the Riversong Kitchen

Use the Freshest Foods Available—Prepare foods that are in season and are grown close to your home. At Riversong, we grow the largest vegetable and herb garden we can tend. Even if you only have time or room for one small pot of herbs in your kitchen window, grow some portion of your own food.

Take Care in Presentation—Whether you serve food on large platters or on individual plates, take a close look at the final product. Don't clutter the plate. Wipe the rim with a clean cloth soaked in vinegar to remove smudges and fingerprints. Plates should be chilled for cold foods and heated for hot foods. Garnishes are important, but everything on the plate should be edible.

Avoid Repeating Textures, Flavors, or Colors on a Plate—I like to have two-thirds of the plate contrast in some way with the other third, either in color or texture. If you have round carrots, cut your potatoes into strips. If you have a rich basil butter on a fillet of fish, add something different to the vegetables. If you are serving white fish, don't serve white cauliflower and white potatoes.

Use the Right Tool for the Job—Invest in good knives and quality pots and pans. Your work in the kitchen will be more efficient and more satisfying.

Cleanliness in All Things—Every cook appreciates a clean kitchen, but that takes constant diligence. Wash your hands often throughout the day. Make sure cutting boards are scrubbed. Wash all homegrown and purchased vegetables and fruit well. Wear a clean apron and tie your hair back while cooking.

Eat Well, Always—We can't control all things in life, but we can usually control what goes into our mouths. Don't let the pace of life rob you of the pleasure and potential for eating well. Eating well doesn't mean fancy. It means fresh, nutritious, natural, and flavorful.

Savory Gruyère Cabbage Loaf

In the deep of Alaska's winter, lettuce is virtually unavailable. Cabbage is the mainstay, lasting all winter in the root cellar. This loaf can be served as a vegetable side dish or an entrée. I like to slice it into 2-inch wedges, dolloped with sour cream, and serve it with smoked pork chops.

1 head green cabbage (2 to
   3 pounds)
3 tablespoons unsalted
   butter
2 tablespoons canola oil
¼ cup diced yellow onion
Salt and freshly ground
   pepper to taste
3 eggs
½ cup heavy cream
½ cup shredded Gruyère
   cheese
1 tablespoon crushed
   caraway seeds
¾ cup fresh rye bread
   crumbs

Preheat the oven to 375 degrees Fahrenheit. Grease a standard (5-by-9-by-3-inch) loaf pan. Wash, dry, and quarter the cabbage. Slice the cabbage into ¼-inch strips.

Heat the butter and oil in a large sauté pan. Add the onion and sauté over medium heat until the onion is slightly translucent, 5 to 7 minutes. Add the cabbage and stir well to coat the contents of the pan with the butter and oil. Cover the pan and simmer until the cabbage is wilted and has released its liquid. Remove the cover and cook over medium-high heat for 2 to 3 minutes to evaporate the moisture in the pan. Remove the cabbage from the heat and season to taste with salt and pepper.

In a medium mixing bowl, beat the eggs and cream together. To the cabbage, add the Gruyère cheese, caraway seeds, egg mixture, and ¼ cup of the rye crumbs. Place the cabbage mixture into the buttered loaf pan. Press the remaining ½ cup rye crumbs onto the top of the loaf. Place the loaf on the middle rack of the oven and bake for 40 to 45 minutes. The loaf should be fairly firm to the touch and golden brown on top. Let stand for 20 minutes before slicing.

Makes 6 to 8 servings.

White Bean Chili

Of course, it makes sense that beans would be popular in Alaska. They are easy to store and keep, and have been predominant in rural Alaskan diets since the gold rush. This white chili is just as hearty as its traditional counterpart, but unusual enough to perk up a winter meal.

2 cups dried Great
   Northern white beans
2 slices bacon, diced
1½ pounds boneless turkey
   breast, shredded
1 large onion, peeled and
   chopped coarsely
2 cloves garlic, peeled and
   minced
½ cup homemade or canned
   chicken stock
1 teaspoon mild (or light)
   chili powder
1 teaspoon ground cumin
1 teaspoon ground
   coriander
Salt and freshly ground
   white pepper to taste
¼ cup shredded Monterey
   jack cheese

Wash and sort the beans. Place the beans in a large saucepan and add 6 cups of cold water. Bring the beans to a rapid boil over high heat. Turn off the heat and cover the pan with a lid. Let sit 1 hour. Drain and rinse the beans and add 6 cups of hot water. Bring to a boil, reduce the heat, and simmer for 1½ hours, or until the beans are just tender.

In a large, heavy stockpot, brown the bacon over medium heat. Add the turkey and brown on all sides. Add the onion and garlic and sauté, stirring frequently, until the onion is softened, about 10 minutes. Add the chicken stock, chili powder, cumin, coriander, and white beans. Simmer over low heat for 30 minutes. Season with salt and pepper to taste. Serve hot, sprinkled with the cheese.

Makes 4 to 6 servings.

Spaghetti Pie with Shredded Carrots

This pie is a good children's dish. When I serve it to adults, I dress it up with Green and Red Tomato Relish (see page 199).

6 ounces uncooked spaghetti
  noodles
¼ cup unsalted butter
1 cup shredded carrot
1 clove garlic, peeled and
  minced
½ cup shredded Parmesan
  cheese
2 eggs, beaten
½ cup shredded sharp
  Cheddar cheese

Preheat the oven to 350 degrees Fahrenheit. Grease a 9-inch pie pan. Bring 4 quarts of salted water to a rapid boil. Add the noodles and cook for 10 to 12 minutes, or until they are al dente. Drain and rinse the noodles well. Place the noodles in a medium mixing bowl.

Melt the butter in a medium skillet over medium heat. Add the carrot and garlic. Sauté for 5 minutes, or until the carrot has softened. Add the carrot to the spaghetti, including any butter remaining in the skillet. Add the Parmesan cheese and the beaten eggs, mixing well.

Press the spaghetti mixture into the pan. Place the pie on the center rack of the oven and bake for 20 minutes. Remove and sprinkle with the Cheddar cheese. Return to the oven until the cheese is bubbly and golden, about 5 minutes. Cut in wedges and serve.

Makes 6 servings.

Beef Braised in Beer

I like this recipe because of the way it is thickened with bread. The dark beer gives the meat a rich flavor. Serve this dish with a crusty French loaf and fried potatoes.

¼ cup canola oil
3 pounds round steak, cut into ½-inch cubes
Salt and freshly ground pepper to taste
1 large slice sourdough bread, crust trimmed
2 tablespoons grainy mustard
3 tablespoons unsalted butter
1 large onion, peeled and thinly sliced
2 tablespoons dark brown sugar
2 tablespoons red wine vinegar
2 cups dark beer

Preheat the oven to 350 degrees Fahrenheit. In a large, oven-proof saucepan or flameproof casserole, heat the oil. Sear the meat on all sides over medium heat. Drain off any excess oil. Season the meat with salt and pepper. Set aside.

Spread the slice of bread with the mustard. In a medium sauté pan, melt the butter. Add the onion and sauté until golden, about 5 minutes. Add the brown sugar and continue to cook until the onion is caramelized. Add the red wine vinegar and continue to sauté until the vinegar is absorbed.

Place the bread slice into the casserole with the beef, sticking it down into the middle of the meat. Add the onion. Heat the beer in the sauté pan and then pour it over the beef. Cover and braise the beef on the center rack of the oven for 4 hours. Serve the beef with the sauce as is, or puree the sauce until smooth.

Makes 6 servings.

Cheddar Cheese Apple Pie

The combination of warm, sharp Cheddar cheese and sweet apples makes this a rich, all-American dessert.

3 tablespoons small pearl
   tapioca
Pinch of salt
1 teaspoon ground
   cinnamon
1 teaspoon ground nutmeg
Juice of 1 lemon
6 large tart green apples
   (such as Granny Smith)
Pastry for a 9-inch double-
   crust mealy pie shell (see
   "Two Kinds of Pie
   Crust" on pages 47
   and 48)
1 cup shredded sharp
   Cheddar cheese
2 tablespoons unsalted
   butter
2 tablespoons heavy cream

Preheat the oven to 400 degrees Fahrenheit. Combine the tapioca, salt, cinnamon, and nutmeg in a medium bowl. Place the lemon juice in a large bowl. Peel, core, and slice the apples and add to the lemon juice as they are cut. Add the spice and tapioca mixture to the apples and juice.

Roll out half of the pastry and line a 9-inch glass or ceramic pie pan with it. Spread the apple mixture onto the pastry. Top with the shredded cheese. Dot with the butter, and sprinkle the cream over the mixture. Sprinkle the rim of the pie shell with a little water to moisten the edge.

Roll out the remaining pastry and place it over the top of the pie. Seal the edges by pinching with your fingertips. Cut slashes in the top crust for steam to escape, and decorate with shapes cut out of the leftover dough, if desired. Brush the crust lightly with cold water. Place the pie on a foil-lined baking sheet. Bake on the center rack of the oven for 45 to 50 minutes, or until the crust is golden brown.

Makes 6 to 8 servings.

Alaska Tea

Alaska tea, sometimes called Russian tea, can be found in various forms all over Alaska. This recipe uses real ingredients, unlike the instant orange drink that is common in parts of Alaska where fresh juice can be hard to find. Not really a tea, it's a delicious hot drink.

1 quart frozen or fresh
   low-bush (or other)
   cranberries
1 2-inch cinnamon stick
3 quarts water
¼ cup lemon juice
2 cups orange juice
2 cups sugar, or to taste

Combine the cranberries and cinnamon stick with the water in a large, nonaluminum saucepan. Simmer uncovered over medium heat until the berries are tender, about 25 minutes. Strain the juice through a double layer of cheesecloth and discard the berries. Add the lemon juice, orange juice, and sugar to the cranberry juice. Return the mixture to the saucepan and heat until sugar is dissolved. Serve hot.

Makes 12 servings, about 3½ quarts.

Winter Cranberries

I like to serve a dollop of this condiment with a spicy kippered salmon patty, brown rice, and fresh, hot sourdough bread. In the summer, add a handful of fresh mint from the garden to the cranberries.

*1½ cups frozen or fresh
  cranberries
½ cup diced red onion
2 tablespoons orange juice
2 dashes hot pepper sauce,
  or to taste*

Chop the cranberries coarsely, either by hand or with a food processor. Add the onion, orange juice, and hot pepper sauce to taste. Mix well. Refrigerate, covered, at least 1 hour before serving. The cranberries will keep 1 week, refrigerated.

Makes 1 cup.

When Friends Drop By

Carl was outside gathering firewood—his endless winter chore. I was inside the cabin going through the tribulations of laundry day, pumping water by hand and heating it to wash the baby's diapers. It was an extremely cold day in late February. Wet, clean clothes hung all over the cabin, releasing a pleasant moisture into the normally dry, wood-heated air. I set about my chores, keeping a watchful eye on the baby so that she wouldn't crawl too close to the wood stove. I was pregnant with our second child and was beginning to have trouble chasing Carly around the cabin.

Carl burst into the cabin amid a flurry of cold air. Stomping the snow off his boots and wiping away the little icicles that had formed on his mustache, he told me that a helicopter had landed in our front yard. Company was coming.

Our visitors were officials for the Iditasport race, the world's longest cross-country ski race. A 300-kilometer trek from Knik to Skwentna and back, the race presents river conditions and winter weather that are challenging to even the most rigorously trained athletes. The officials had decided they needed more frequent checkpoints along the Yentna River and had stopped in to ask if we would mind providing shelter for a few hours. We didn't mind in the least.

We started a fire in the unfinished lodge. Carl had been working on the building every day to have it ready for guests by May. It was far from completed but would do as an impromptu checkpoint for the race.

We knew the skiers would be wet from traveling in the deep snow, so we strung up line for drying their gloves and socks. I was busy grinding coffee beans and heating water when one of the race officials mentioned that he had been dreaming of blueberry pie.

At the time I was working my way through a cookbook called *Pastries and Pies, Savory and Sweet* by Bernard Clayton. Clayton probably would have been amused if he could have seen me peering into his book by kerosene lamp in that little cabin. I was trying to decide whether to dig out a frozen block of butter that was harder than diamonds from our pantry on the porch or to use the soft goo that occupied the butter dish on the table. Clayton's book had taught me that the fat used in a pie crust must stay cold. I learned that night that a tightly insulated, overheated cabin in Alaska is a tough place to make good pie dough. Thank goodness for the mound of snow outside the front door.

Our visitors had just skied a rigorous 120 miles in below-zero weather and had nearly as many more miles before the race was over, so they were delighted with the warm, sweet pie. They acted as though I had worked a miracle. I discovered the joy of cooking for people I didn't know.

After we cleaned up the dishes, and the last skier's headlamp twinkled in the darkness as its wearer moved away from us, Carl and I sat thinking about how pleasant it was to have company drop in.

In April, two months after the Iditasport race—and the day after our daughter Amanda was born—we moved into the beautiful new lodge that Carl had worked on so hard all winter.

Smoked Pork Chops with Braised Sauerkraut and Apples

This quick dish is my fast-food recipe. It has pulled me through some last-minute guest arrivals more than once. I try always to have a case of smoked pork chops in the freezer.

6 smoked pork chops,
½-inch thick
Salt and freshly ground
pepper to taste
3 tablespoons unsalted
butter
2 medium onions, peeled
and sliced into thin rings
2 medium tart green apples
(such as Granny Smith),
peeled, cored, and sliced
thin lengthwise
1 quart (4 cups) sauerkraut
2½ cups homemade or
canned chicken stock
1 tablespoon caraway seeds

Preheat the oven to 350 degrees Fahrenheit. Sprinkle the pork chops with salt and pepper. Heat the butter in a large skillet over medium heat. Add the pork chops and brown, turning once. Remove the chops and keep warm.

Add the onions and apples to the skillet, adding a little more butter if needed. Sauté until the onions are softened. Remove the pan from the heat. Remove the apples and onions from the skillet.

Drain and rinse the sauerkraut. Press out any extra moisture. Place the sauerkraut and ½ cup of the chicken stock in the skillet and simmer over medium heat until the stock reduces. The sauerkraut should wilt a little as it cooks. Sprinkle with a little of the caraway seeds.

Turn the sauerkraut into a large, buttered, oven-proof casserole. Arrange the pork chops on top of the sauerkraut. Spread the onion and apple mixture on top of the pork. Pour the remaining 2 cups chicken stock over all. Sprinkle the remaining caraway seeds on top. Cover the casserole with a lid or aluminum foil. Place on the center rack of the oven. Bake for 25 minutes, or until the excess moisture is absorbed.

Makes 4 to 6 servings.

Smoked Salmon Pizza

Over the past decade, this recipe has been made at the lodge more than any other. We prepare our own dough at the lodge but have simplified the recipe here for you.

3 tablespoons olive oil

1 clove minced garlic

4 cups peeled, seeded, and chopped tomatoes

1 teaspoon dried oregano

1 teaspoon dried basil

1 teaspoon crushed fennel seeds

1 tablespoon unsalted butter

6 cups blanched broccoli, coarsely chopped

Salt and freshly ground pepper to taste

2½ cups shredded mozzarella cheese

1 12-inch prepared Italian bread shell

¼ cup shredded Parmesan cheese

¼ pound kippered salmon, sliced into strips

Heat the oil in a sauté pan. Add the garlic and cook for 1 minute. Add the tomatoes and simmer gently until thickened, about 30 minutes. Stir in the herbs and fennel seeds. Set the tomato mixture aside to cool.

Melt the butter over medium heat and add the broccoli. Heat until the broccoli has softened, about 5 minutes. Season with salt and pepper and set aside.

Preheat the oven to 425 degrees Fahrenheit. Spread 1 cup of the mozzarella cheese over the Italian bread shell. Spoon the tomato mixture over the cheese. Add the broccoli. Combine the Parmesan cheese with the remaining 1½ cups mozzarella, and sprinkle over the broccoli. Arrange the kippered salmon slices in a circular pattern on top. Bake on the center rack of the oven for 15 to 20 minutes, until the cheese is bubbly and brown. Serve the pizza warm.

Makes 8 to 10 servings.

Kirsten's Winter Goose

This goose is stuffed with apples and onions, and slowly roasted in a wine-soaked wrapping of cheesecloth. We don't wait for holidays to serve this winter favorite.

*1 young goose, 9 to
  11 pounds*
Juice of 1 lemon
Salt
*2 apples, peeled and
  quartered*
*2 onions, peeled and
  quartered*
*1 large carrot, peeled and
  coarsely chopped*
*1 celery stalk, peeled and
  coarsely chopped*
*About 2½ cups good-quality
  dry white wine*
1½ tablespoons cornstarch
½ cup port

Remove any excess fat from the rear of the goose. Chop off the wings below the elbow. Rub the goose inside and out with lemon juice. Lightly salt the body cavity.

To secure the wings, run a large skewer through the carcass at the shoulder. Run another skewer through the hips to secure the legs. Use string to tie the legs together against the tail.

Taking care not to pierce the flesh, prick the skin with a sharp knife in several places near the lower breast and thighs. This will help release the excess fat. Place the goose, breast side up, on a rack in a large roasting pan with a cover. Add 1 inch of water to the pan. Place the pan over a burner, bring the water to a boil, and cover. Reduce the heat and simmer 45 minutes, adding water as needed.

Preheat the oven to 325 degrees Fahrenheit. Remove the goose from the pan and drain off the liquid. Much of the liquid is fat, which can be cooled and saved, if desired. Remove the hip skewer and loosely stuff the cavity with apples and onions. Replace the skewer. Wrap the goose securely in cheesecloth that has been soaked in white wine. Lay the goose on a rack in a roasting pan, breast side down. Add the carrot and celery, along with any leftover apples and onions, to the

continued on next page

pan. Pour in 1 cup of the white wine. Cover tightly and place in the oven on the center rack. Roast for 1 to 1½ hours, basting frequently with the remaining white wine and accumulated juices.

Uncover the goose, remove the cheesecloth, turn the goose breast side up and baste well. Continue to roast an additional 20 minutes, or until the goose is a rich golden brown. Remove the goose from the pan and set aside on a carving platter. Discard the apples and onions from the cavity.

Skim the fat from the pan juices and strain. Place the juices in a saucepan. Mix the cornstarch and port and add to the saucepan. Simmer on the stove, stirring well. Add white wine if more liquid is needed. Simmer until thickened, skimming off any fat. Serve with the goose.

Makes 8 to 10 servings.

Pennies from Heaven

This is a simple, fun project for children on a spring day when snow is still on the ground.

1 cup Alaska fireweed
* honey or other honey*
½ cup water

Heat the honey and water in a heavy saucepan. Bring the mixture to a boil until it tests 240 degrees Fahrenheit on a candy thermometer. Drop the honey by teaspoonfuls into fresh, clean snow or into a bucket of cracked ice. The candies will be small, round disks. Store in an airtight container or wrap in plastic wrap.

Makes 30 to 40 candies.

Winter Blueberry-Cranberry Pie

This pie has cranberries added, which give it an unusually rich flavor. I always thicken pies with tapioca rather than cornstarch because tapioca thickens without making the fruit cloudy.

2 cups whole frozen blueberries, thawed and drained

2 cups whole frozen cranberries, thawed and drained

1 cup sugar

3 tablespoons tapioca

Pinch of salt

Pastry for a 9-inch double-crust mealy pie shell (see pages 47 and 48)

2 tablespoons unsalted butter

Preheat the oven to 400 degrees Fahrenheit. Place the blueberries and cranberries in a large bowl. Combine the sugar, tapioca, and salt, and stir into the mixed berries.

Roll out half of the pastry and line a 9-inch glass or ceramic pie pan with it. Spread the fruit mixture onto the pastry. Dot with butter. Sprinkle the rim of the pie shell with a little water to moisten the edge.

Roll out the remaining pastry and place it over the top of the pie. Seal the edges by pinching with your fingertips or crimping with a fork. Cut slashes in the top crust for steam to escape, and decorate with shapes cut out of any leftover dough. Brush the crust lightly with cold water. Place the pie on a foil-lined baking sheet. Bake on the center rack of the oven for 45 to 50 minutes, or until the crust is golden brown.

Makes 6 to 8 servings.

Two Kinds of Pie Crust

We make two kinds of pie crust at Riversong. One is a flaky crust and the other is a mealy crust. The difference lies in how the fat is blended in with the flour.

Flaky pie crusts are used for top crusts and prebaked shells, or when the filling isn't so moist that it will soak the dough and make it soggy. For flaky dough, rub the butter into the flour with your fingers until it is about the size of peas. The flour is not completely blended with the butter. When water is added, the gluten in the flour develops. When the dough is rolled out, the wet flour is flattened and layered between the butter.

Mealy pie crusts are used when the pie filling is very liquid and you want the bottom to resist soaking. For mealy dough, blend the butter into the flour more thoroughly, until it looks like cornmeal.

See page 48 for the Master Pie Crust Recipe.

Master Pie Crust Recipe

This recipe uses the classic method of pie dough preparation. If you prefer, you may mix the dough in a bowl, using a pastry blender.

2 cups all-purpose flour
1 teaspoon salt
1 cup cold unsalted butter
½ cup ice water

Mix the flour and salt together and place on a counter top. Cut the butter into 1-inch pieces. Rub the butter and flour between your fingertips until the mixture is the desired texture (pea-sized for a flaky crust, cornmeal texture for a mealy crust). Add the cold water, a tablespoon at a time, until the dough is just moist enough to form a ball. Flatten the dough with the heel of your hand to layer the butter and flour. Refrigerate for 30 minutes before rolling out.

Makes one 8- or 9-inch double-crust pie shell or two single-crust shells.

Danish Cardamom Cookies

I'm crazy about cardamom, probably because of my Scandinavian heritage. Too much cardamom can produce a bitter taste, so don't increase the amount of cardamom called for in most recipes.

1 cup unsalted butter, at room temperature
½ cup granulated sugar
4 teaspoons ground cardamom
2 cups all-purpose flour
½ teaspoon salt
½ cup sliced almonds
½ cup powdered sugar
1 teaspoon finely minced lemon peel
Sliced almonds, for cookie tops

Preheat the oven to 375 degrees Fahrenheit. Grease a cookie sheet.

Beat the butter, granulated sugar, and the cardamom in a medium bowl until fluffy. Sift together the flour and salt, and add to the butter mixture. Stir in the almonds. Combine the powdered sugar and the lemon peel.

Form 1 tablespoon of the cookie dough into a ball. Roll it in the powdered sugar mixture. Place the ball on the prepared cookie sheet, and flatten it with the bottom of a glass that has been dipped in the powdered sugar. Press a few sliced almonds onto the top of the cookie. Repeat with the remaining cookie dough, spacing the cookies 1 inch apart.

Bake on the center rack of the oven until the cookies are light brown, about 15 minutes. Remove the cookies from the oven and cool completely on a rack before serving.

Makes about 24 cookies.

Lemon Cheese Strudel

This is a very delicate dessert that can be served any time of year. If you are watching calories, try spraying the phyllo dough layers with butter-flavored cooking spray rather than brushing them with butter. Lemon curd can be purchased in the jam section of your market.

1 teaspoon ground
cinnamon
½ cup sugar
3 ounces cream cheese,
softened
¼ teaspoon lemon extract
8 sheets frozen phyllo dough
pastry, thawed
½ cup unsalted butter,
melted
1 cup lemon curd

Combine the cinnamon and the sugar in a small bowl. Set aside. Blend together the cream cheese and lemon extract.

Preheat the oven to 375 degrees Fahrenheit. Grease a cookie sheet. Place 1 phyllo sheet on a work surface (keep the remaining sheets covered). Brush the sheet with some of the melted butter and sprinkle with 2 teaspoons of the cinnamon sugar. Top the buttered phyllo sheet with a new sheet. Butter the second sheet and sprinkle with sugar. Repeat the process, using the remaining 6 phyllo sheets.

Spread the cream cheese onto the pastry, leaving at least a ½-inch border on all sides of the filling. Spread the lemon curd on top of the cream cheese. Fold the short ends over the filling. Brush the edges with melted butter. Roll up the phyllo dough starting at the long side. Brush with melted butter. Press the seam to seal.

Place the strudel seam side down on the prepared cookie sheet. Brush strudel with butter and sprinkle with 1 tablespoon of the cinnamon sugar. Bake until golden and crisp, about 20 minutes. Cool slightly. Cut into slices with a sharp serrated knife.

Makes 6 servings.

Real Hot Chocolate

It amazes me how many people love this drink and how few have ever had the real thing, as opposed to the packaged version. I'm sure we've won culinary acclaim among our younger guests because of our hot chocolate alone.

1 cup heavy cream
4 cups milk
1 teaspoon vanilla extract
6 ounces bittersweet
  chocolate, finely chopped
Heavy cream, whipped

Heat the heavy cream, milk, and vanilla in a medium saucepan over medium heat, just to the point of boiling. Remove from the heat, add the chocolate, and whisk until the chocolate has melted. Whirl the milk and chocolate mixture on medium-high speed in a blender to make it frothy. Serve in mugs with a dollop of whipped cream.

Makes 4 servings, about 6 cups.

Mulled Wine

A sprinkling of guests brave the Alaska winter to visit Riversong. When they come, we offer a hot spiced wine while we look for spectacular northern lights overhead. This drink will simmer perfectly on a wood stove. Note that the spiced syrup should be made a day ahead of time.

Peel of 2 oranges
1 2-inch cinnamon stick,
  chopped in half
4 whole cloves
2 whole cardamom pods
½ teaspoon ground nutmeg
1 cup light brown sugar
1½ cups water
1 bottle (750 ml) dry red
  wine

Preheat the oven to 350 degrees Fahrenheit. Remove the white pith from the orange peels and cut the peels into strips. Place on a baking sheet and bake for 5 minutes. Remove the peels from the oven and chop fine. Make a cheesecloth pouch for the peels, the two pieces of cinnamon stick, cloves, cardamom, and nutmeg. Tie the pouch securely with unwaxed string.

Place the pouch in a small pan with the brown sugar and the water. Cover and simmer slowly for 10 minutes. Allow to cool and keep covered for 24 hours.

When ready to serve, heat the wine only until the surface shimmers slightly. Don't allow to boil. Remove the seasoning pouch from the syrup and add the syrup to the wine. Serve the hot spiced wine in warmed mugs.

Makes 4 to 6 servings, about 5 cups.

On Moose

One of my favorite views is from our bedroom window in winter. I can see across the garden and beyond to the Yentna River. At night, the contrast of the white snow against the dark night sets a dramatic scene. And the *stars*. There must be more stars shining over Riversong than anywhere else in the world. The brilliant celestial canvas seems to go on forever.

One night I looked out our bedroom window to find a huge male moose standing right below me. Quiet and slow moving, he was nibbling at the branches of a sturdy tree called a mayday that sits on a small knoll at the edge of the garden. The mayday tree blossoms with a lovely little white flower that smells sweet and scatters over the garden in the summer, usually much later than the first of May in our locale. In the winter, the tree stands barren against the moonlight, appreciated only by a few wandering moose.

My midnight visitor stood quietly for a long time, munching slowly at the small branches of the trees near the front of our cabin. How could those little branches be of interest to such a large animal?

It seemed strange to be so close to this enormous moose, without his knowing I was there. I've had the same experience from my window with bears, beavers, eagles, and other Alaska wildlife, but moose fascinate me the most. We see them most often when the snow is the deepest and they travel the river in search of food. They remind me of huge sailing ships gliding along the frozen river.

We have a strange shared existence with the moose that pass along our trails in winter. We view them as docile, wild animals that have a certain ungainly beauty and an almost sad charm to them. But they are also capable of tremendous harm to an unwary person. One has only to look at Carl's prized snow machine, named "Black Beauty" by the girls, to see what a moose can do with a few powerful kicks.

One day, Carl and the girls were riding Black Beauty through the woods behind our house when they came upon a moose, who became disgruntled at having to share his trail with a strange, roaring black creature. The moose charged the intruder, then turned again and charged a second time, giving the machine a very firm and defiant kick to the headlamp and windshield. Carl covered the girls with his body at the rear of the machine in the snow. Luckily, no one was injured.

Poor Carl—he likes to keep our equipment looking new for as long as he can. Black Beauty, although lovingly cared for by its owner, now looks a little rough. Not only have various moose taken to bashing it, but a goose decided to peck out the foam padding of the seats for nesting material.

In our household, we eat moose meat like many people eat beef. Each year, we hunt a moose that will feed us for the whole winter. Sometimes we make a special trip to the west and take a caribou. After a steady diet of moose or caribou, regular beef tastes fatty and even slightly rancid. Moose meat isn't gamy at all if cared for properly. On cold winter days, Carl appreciates the opportunity to take breaks from his outdoor chores and warm up in the lodge. I serve him a warm bowl of stew by the wood stove. Carl always eats moose stew with a particular gusto. I think he secretly relishes just the tiniest bit of revenge for battles lost along the trail.

Smoked Salmon Cardamom Spread

Smoked salmon, sour cream, and cardamom is a flavor blend I discovered one day by accident. We chill champagne in the snow to serve with this spread for a special winter appetizer.

1 pound kippered salmon
¾ cup sour cream
½ teaspoon ground
*   cardamom*
Freshly ground pepper to
*   taste*
1 lemon

Chop half of the kippered salmon in the bowl of a food processor. Add the sour cream, cardamom, and pepper. Grate the zest of the lemon into the salmon mixture. Squeeze one-half of the lemon's juices into the mixture as well. Process the salmon mixture until it is pureed. Transfer the puree to a large bowl. Coarsely chop the remaining salmon and add it to the puree. Mix well, cover, and refrigerate until serving time. (Other flavorings, such as fresh chopped basil, cayenne pepper, or sun-dried tomatoes, can be substituted for the cardamom.) Serve a dollop of spread on favorite crackers or bread.

Makes 1½ pounds (24 1-ounce servings).

Marilyn's Potato Rye Bread

Marilyn Pierce-Bulger, a friend of mine, is a very fine cook. She shared this recipe with us years ago and we are still making it at the lodge. It is dense, and the anise seeds and molasses give it a slightly nutty flavor.

1 cup warm potato water (110 to 115 degrees Fahrenheit); use the water left from boiling potatoes
1½ packages (1½ tablespoons) active dry yeast
⅓ cup dark molasses
1 tablespoon salt
1 tablespoon anise seeds
¼ cup shortening
2 cups rye flour (medium)
¼ cup bran
4 to 5 cups all-purpose flour

Place the warm potato water in a large bowl. Dissolve the yeast in the warm water. Let the mixture proof for 5 to 10 minutes, or until the yeast is slightly bubbly. Stir in the molasses, salt, anise seeds, shortening, rye flour, and bran. Add enough all-purpose flour to make a kneadable dough. Knead the dough for 8 to 10 minutes. Place the dough in a large, oiled bowl and let rise in a warm place until doubled in bulk.

Punch down the dough and divide in half. Shape into round, flattish loaves and place in greased pie pans. Let the dough rise again until doubled. Preheat the oven to 375 degrees Fahrenheit and bake for 30 to 35 minutes, or until the loaves sound hollow when tapped and are golden on the bottom. Remove from the oven and cool on a rack before slicing.

Makes 2 round loaves.

Reindeer Sausage Soup

This is a hearty meat-and-vegetable soup. Reindeer sausage can be purchased by mail order through Alaskan meat companies. It is lean and spicy.

1 teaspoon fresh thyme, or
½ teaspoon dried
1 teaspoon salt
1½ teaspoons hot pepper
sauce
1 bay leaf
8 cups homemade or canned
beef stock
1 medium-sized green
cabbage, coarsely
shredded
2 large onions, peeled and
thinly sliced
3 large carrots, peeled and
sliced ½ inch thick
1 cup green beans, cut into
½-inch pieces
½ cup green peas
3 large potatoes, cut into
½-inch cubes
1 celery stalk, sliced ½ inch
thick
1 pound Alaska reindeer
sausage, sliced ½ inch
thick
1 cup sourdough bread
croutons

Place the thyme, salt, hot pepper sauce, and bay leaf into a large saucepan. Pour in the beef stock. Stir well and place the pan over high heat. Bring the stock to a boil, stirring well. Add the cabbage, onions, carrots, beans, peas, potatoes, and celery. Bring the soup back to a boil. Reduce the heat and simmer for 40 minutes. Add the sausage and simmer for an additional 15 to 20 minutes.

Remove the soup from the heat, ladle into individual serving bowls or a soup tureen, and garnish with the sourdough croutons.

Makes 6 to 8 servings.

Potato Pancake with Carrots and Onion

If we are lucky enough to have imported caviar in the house, I like to serve this pancake in wedges, with a generous dollop of sour cream and a teaspoon of caviar.

2 eggs
3 cups shredded potatoes
½ cup shredded carrot
1 small red onion, coarsely chopped
1 clove garlic, peeled and minced
Salt and freshly ground pepper to taste
¼ cup unsalted butter, melted

Beat the eggs in a medium bowl. Add the potatoes, carrot, onion, and garlic. Season with salt and pepper to taste. Pour half of the melted butter into a nonstick 12-inch skillet so that it is ⅛ inch deep. Add the potato mixture and cook without disturbing for 5 to 7 minutes, or until the potatoes have formed a golden crust. Slip the pancake out onto a plate, add the remaining butter, and then return the pancake to the skillet, flipping it to cook the other side. Continue to cook until golden, approximately 10 minutes. Serve hot.

Makes 6 to 8 servings.

Pleasures of the Winter Kitchen

The wintertime kitchen at Riversong differs from the summer kitchen. Because we have fewer guests in winter, the atmosphere in the kitchen is more participatory. We have a buffet near the pantry where guests can sit on high stools and observe us cooking from a safe distance. Or, often, they put on aprons and help peel carrots or potatoes.

Sometimes at night, when we are viewing northern lights, we chill a bottle of champagne in the snow outside the kitchen door. When it is well frosted, we bring the icy champagne into the warm lodge. I like to share our summer-caught smoked salmon with our winter guests, who can't imagine this frozen place any way other than lying deep in ice and snow.

I like to serve meals in the kitchen in winter. We put candles all around the big work table in the center of the room and I place a colorful cotton runner down the center. We lay out the food buffet-style. Our guests seem to enjoy the intimacy of being invited into our kitchen.

Winter is a time of hearty meals shared around the wood stove. We pull chairs up to the stove and balance our plates on our knees. Long, tall tales last well into the night as we stay warm.

Green Cabbage Salad

I love the flavors of cabbage, blue cheese, apples, raisins, and onions all mixed together. This salad is like a cole slaw. We serve it primarily in winter, accompanied by pureed root vegetables or mashed potatoes, slices of honey-basted ham, and fresh biscuits.

1 large head green cabbage
1 cup fresh mayonnaise
½ cup crumbled blue cheese
Half a red onion, diced
¼ cup golden raisins
½ cup shredded Parmesan
* cheese*
1 large tart green apple
* (such as Granny Smith),*
* peeled, cored, and diced*

Finely shred the cabbage into a large bowl. Toss with the remaining ingredients and serve slightly chilled.

Makes 4 to 6 servings.

Riversong Moose Stew

Many people who have visited the lodge over the winter have tasted this stew. I like to serve it with white rice and corn bread. Moose meat is our favorite meat because of its lean texture and rich flavor. It is still difficult to acquire commercially. Beef can be substituted.

6 strips of bacon, cut into pieces
2½ to 3 pounds moose meat, cut into 1-inch cubes
Salt and freshly ground pepper to taste
3 tablespoons all-purpose flour
1 large onion, peeled and coarsely chopped
2 cups dry red wine
1 cup homemade or canned beef stock
3 tablespoons brandy
2 cloves garlic, peeled and minced
½ teaspoon dried marjoram
½ teaspoon dried thyme
Half an orange, washed
6 whole cloves
2 tablespoons unsalted butter
3 large carrots, peeled and coarsely chopped
½ pound mushrooms, coarsely chopped

Preheat the oven to 350 degrees Fahrenheit. In an oven-safe 3-quart casserole, cook the bacon over medium heat until brown. Remove the bacon with a slotted spoon, drain, and set aside.

Sprinkle the moose meat with salt and pepper. Dredge it in the flour. Add the meat to the pan drippings. Brown on all sides over medium heat.

Add the reserved bacon, onion, wine, stock, brandy, garlic, marjoram, and thyme. Stir until the sauce thickens and is bubbly. Stud the orange with the cloves and tuck it into the liquid. Cover the casserole and place it on the center rack of the oven. Bake for 2 to 2½ hours.

In a large skillet, melt the butter over medium heat. Add the carrots and mushrooms and cook until tender. Set aside. When the stew is done, add the carrots and mushrooms, cover, and return to the oven for 5 minutes. Remove the orange and discard. Serve immediately.

Makes 4 to 6 servings.

Moose Meatballs

As with the other moose recipes in this collection, if you don't have moose meat, substitute beef—or move to Alaska! I like to use dehydrated onion bits because they remain slightly crisp on the surface of the meatballs. Serve the meatballs with wide egg noodles or rice.

1 pound ground moose meat

1 large tart green apple
   (such as Granny Smith),
   peeled, cored, and
   shredded

Salt and freshly ground
   pepper to taste

3 tablespoons dehydrated
   onion bits

½ cup Italian seasoned
   bread crumbs

3 tablespoons olive oil

¾ cup dry red wine

¼ cup water

2 8-ounce cans tomato sauce

1 teaspoon dried rosemary

In a large bowl, combine the moose meat, apple, salt, pepper, and onion bits. Mix and shape into 1-inch balls. Roll the balls in the bread crumbs. Heat the oil in a large, heavy skillet. Add the meatballs and cook over medium heat until evenly browned. Drain off any excess oil.

Mix together wine, water, tomato sauce, and rosemary. Pour over the meatballs, cover, and simmer 20 to 30 minutes. Serve warm.

Makes 16 to 20 meatballs, 4 to 6 servings.

Caribou Swiss Steak

My mother often made Swiss steak when I was a child. I loved the aromatic combined flavors of apples, onions, and long-simmered meats. If you have to, substitute beef for the caribou. Caribou is a wonderfully lean and flavorful, but not gamy, meat.

2 pounds caribou round
steaks
½ cup all-purpose flour
Salt and freshly ground
pepper to taste
3 tablespoons bacon fat
1 cup chopped wild
mushrooms
1 medium onion, sliced and
separated into rings
1 large tart green apple
(such as Granny Smith),
peeled, cored, and
chopped
1 clove garlic, peeled and
minced
¼ cup sherry

Pound the caribou steaks thin. Combine the flour, salt, and pepper in a shallow dish. Dredge the meat in the flour mixture, shaking off any excess. Heat the bacon fat in a large, heavy skillet. Add the meat and brown on both sides. Drain off any excess fat. Add the mushrooms, onion, apple, garlic, and sherry. Cover and simmer over medium heat for 1½ hours or until tender. If more liquid is needed, add some water or chicken stock.

Makes 4 servings.

Baked Apples

Fruits have usually lost their freshness by the time supplies are purchased, sit on the airplane dock half the day, fly to the lodge, are unloaded, and are brought to the kitchen. But we can count on apples making the journey in decent shape. The combination of nuts, butter, and sourdough bread crumbs baked in a luscious, sweet apple makes this dessert a winter favorite.

½ cup dried currants, soaked in hot water to plump
½ cup finely ground walnuts
⅔ cup sugar
1 teaspoon ground cinnamon
⅛ teaspoon ground nutmeg
¼ cup sourdough bread crumbs
2 tablespoons Calvados or applejack
6 large red cooking apples (such as Braeburn), cored
¼ cup unsalted butter
Heavy cream

Preheat the oven to 325 degrees Fahrenheit. Butter a baking dish large enough to hold the apples. In a small bowl, mix the currants, walnuts, sugar, cinnamon, nutmeg, bread crumbs, and Calvados. The mixture should have a fairly fine texture.

Pack the center of each apple with some of the mixture, and then, using a wide spatula, place the apples in the baking dish. Push a small piece of the butter into the top of each apple. Pour 1 cup of water into the baking dish and cover with aluminum foil. Bake in the center of the oven for 20 minutes. Remove the foil and baste the apples with the liquid. Cover again loosely with the foil and bake 1 hour longer, basting every 15 minutes. Serve warm with a small bowl of warm heavy cream for diners to spoon over the apples.

Makes 6 servings.

Sage and Onion Sauce

Try adding different flavors to this sauce, such as other herbs, hot pepper sauce, or beef stock. The possible combinations are almost endless. I love this sauce just the way it is, served with smoked pork chops and spicy apple rings. It goes well with any pork or poultry dish.

¼ cup unsalted butter
2 medium yellow onions,
*   peeled and thinly sliced*
2 teaspoons dried sage
*   leaves, crumbled*
¼ cup heavy cream

Melt the butter in a medium sauté pan. Add the onions and sage. Sauté until the onions are soft and golden, but not brown. Stir in the cream and serve.

Makes 1 cup.

Northern Days, Northern Nights

The snow was deep on the ground. Although the morning was well under way, the sun hadn't come up yet. Carl had been up for hours, first stoking the wood stove, then heating water for the morning coffee. The wood stove, standing in the center of the main room of the lodge, had been burning brightly for months. By kerosene lantern, Carl had run through his morning mental checklist. (The electric generator is a luxury in the winter and is seldom turned on.) He ground coffee beans slowly by hand as he sat by the wood stove. Coffee made, breakfast started, he dressed for the outside: first his insulated overalls, then his white arctic winter boots, wool cap, and large mittens. He checked all the animals and kicked the ice out of their water bowls before returning to the cabin. The air was astringent, and silence permeated the grounds.

Inside the lodge, I made my way out of the layers of down comforters on our bed and, dressing warmly, I went downstairs. The sun cast a pink glow on the windows. Soon the girls awoke. It was not hard to tell when they were coming.

With a resounding thump, Carly jumped from her bunk bed, quickly followed by Amanda, and the house sprang to life. The girls flew down the stairs and I could feel their energy fill the room. They talked a mile a minute, asking for breakfast, posing impossible questions. So began a winter day at Riversong.

I turned on the two big propane ovens to get them started and to help warm the room. A large hardwood work table commands the center of the kitchen. I dumped ingredients for bread into a big plastic bucket and stirred them with a long wooden paddle. Then the dough sat near the stoves for an hour, covered with a cotton towel. In the winter, I use a bread recipe that allows the dough to rise three times. In the summer, the pace of the kitchen is quick, and bread only rises twice. The batter bubbles up in the plastic bucket like a cauldron of magic potion. Most people write that kneading is the most pleasurable part of bread making, but for me it's the bubbling in the big bucket.

The girls worked on projects in the kitchen or upstairs, where it was a little warmer. When they were done, we made chocolate chip cookies together in the kitchen.

The sun went down around 4:30 P.M. We ate early so that we weren't in the kitchen late. It's a winter ritual because the temperatures plummet as night approaches. Unused rooms have been closed off, returning the lodge to a one-room cabin heated only by a wood stove. A warm bowl of stew, freshly baked bread, and a lot of cookies fueled us for the cold night ahead.

After the busy day, we sat around the wood stove, enjoying simple pleasures. Carl played the guitar and the girls sang along. We darkened the cabin and looked up at the sky. The northern lights came out. Streaks of color shimmered and danced across the star-studded vastness. Blues and greens, reds and pinks flashed in curtains that seemed to engulf us. We felt tiny as we watched the sky open up.

The lights of Alaska, from the very first glint of dawn until our late-night displays of northern lights, measure all our days.

Riversong Winter Soup

This soup is Danish in origin. It is a sweet onion, apple, and cream combination that is perfect for a winter's day. Serve it with open-face grilled sausage sandwiches.

½ cup unsalted butter
1 large yellow onion,
   peeled, thinly sliced, and
   separated into rings
4 large tart green apples
   (such as Granny Smith),
   peeled, cored, and
   coarsely chopped
3 cups homemade or canned
   chicken stock
1 cup heavy cream
2 tablespoons Calvados or
   applejack
Salt and freshly ground
   white pepper to taste

In a large saucepan, melt the butter over medium heat and sauté the onion until golden and softened, about 10 minutes. Add the apples and continue to sauté for an additional 10 minutes. Add the chicken stock, cream, and Calvados. Bring the mixture to a boil, reduce the heat, and simmer for 20 minutes. Season with salt and pepper.

Makes 4 servings.

Sourdough Soup

The idea for this soup came from the French version of onion soup. The tomato-garlic garnish can be added to taste.

½ cup unsalted butter
12 large slices sourdough bread
12 slices Danish white cheese (¼ inch thick), such as Danbo
8 cups homemade or canned beef stock
1 tomato, blanched, peeled, seeded, and chopped
1 clove garlic, peeled and minced

Preheat the oven to 350 degrees Fahrenheit. In a large skillet, melt the butter. Fry each slice of bread in the butter on both sides until crisp. Remove the pan from the heat and set aside. Drain the bread on paper towels. Place the bread in a 4-quart casserole or oven-proof soup bowl. Place a slice of cheese on each piece of bread.

Heat the beef stock to a boil and pour over the bread and cheese. Place the casserole in the oven and bake for 10 to 15 minutes, or until the cheese has melted.

Meanwhile, add the tomato and garlic to the skillet and sauté until any moisture from the tomatoes is absorbed and the garlic is aromatic. Serve the soup in individual bowls, or family-style, with a dollop of tomato-garlic garnish.

Makes 4 to 6 servings.

Sourdough Bread

We make a variety of bread and rolls at Riversong every day. Of course, guests are curious about the famous Alaska sourdough, and we serve it often. Our recipe for Sourdough Starter is found on page 78.

1 package (1 tablespoon) quick-rise active dry yeast
¾ cup warm water
½ cup sourdough starter, at room temperature (see page 78)
3 to 4 cups all-purpose flour
1 teaspoon honey
1 teaspoon salt
2 teaspoons unsalted butter, melted
1 egg, lightly beaten
Melted unsalted butter (optional)

In a large mixing bowl, combine the yeast, water, starter, 2 cups of the flour, honey, and salt. Let sit for 5 minutes. Beat until the dough is smooth. Cover lightly with a towel, and let rise in a warm place until doubled in bulk, about 1 hour.

Stir the dough down with a wooden spoon and then beat in the butter and egg. With an electric mixer equipped with a dough hook, or by hand, beat and knead in the remaining flour to make a soft dough. Continue to beat or knead the sticky dough for about 10 minutes.

Butter a large bowl. Place the dough in the prepared bowl, turning it to butter the top. Cover lightly with a towel and let rise in a warm place until doubled, about 1 hour.

Butter a baking sheet. Punch down the dough and shape into loaves or rolls. Place the bread on the baking sheet and let rise again until doubled, about 40 minutes. Preheat the oven to 400 degrees Fahrenheit. Brush the bread with melted butter, if desired. Bake loaves for 15 minutes, then reduce oven temperature to 375 degrees Fahrenheit, and continue to bake for 15 to 20 minutes. Bake rolls at 400 degrees Fahrenheit for 10 to 15 minutes or until light golden.

Makes 1 rounded loaf, 2 long narrow loaves, or 15 rolls.

Karen's German Onion Bread

This recipe comes from our friend Karen Datzmann, who visits nearly every year from Germany. We love to make this recipe in the winter, when hearty breads are especially delicious.

1 cup tepid water

1½ cups flat beer, at room temperature

⅓ cup light molasses

2 packages (2 tablespoons) quick-rise active dry yeast

2 tablespoons unsalted butter

1 large onion, peeled and chopped

3 cups rye flour (medium)

5 to 7 cups all-purpose flour

1 tablespoon salt

1 egg white, beaten (optional)

In a large bowl, combine the water, beer, molasses, and yeast. Melt the butter in a medium skillet. Add the onion and sauté until translucent. Add the onion to the yeast/beer mixture and then blend in the rye flour, 5 cups of the all-purpose flour, and salt. Mix well and knead the dough for about 10 minutes, adding more all-purpose flour as necessary. The dough will be a little sticky but should be kneadable. Let the dough rest for 15 minutes. Divide the dough in half and knead again for 5 minutes. Shape into rounded loaves and turn out onto a large, well-greased baking sheet. Cover and let rise in a warm place until doubled, about 45 to 55 minutes.

Preheat the oven to 400 degrees Fahrenheit. Brush the dough with egg white or water, if desired. Bake for 35 to 50 minutes, or until the loaves sound hollow when tapped and are golden brown on the bottom.

Makes 2 round loaves.

Smoked Duck Reuben Sandwiches

If you have any Smoked Duck (see page 75) left over, here's something different to try. The flavorful combination of smoky duck, caraway seeds, cheese, and rye has become a lodge favorite.

6 tablespoons unsalted
  butter
1 cup sauerkraut
½ cup homemade or canned
  chicken stock
1 tablespoon caraway seeds
8 slices rye bread
8 tablespoons Russian
  dressing
1½ pounds smoked duck
  meat, shredded
Salt and freshly ground
  pepper to taste
8 tablespoons cranberry
  sauce
8 slices Swiss cheese

Preheat the broiler. Melt 3 tablespoons of the butter in a wide sauté pan over medium heat. Rinse the sauerkraut and squeeze dry. Place the sauerkraut in the pan and sauté for 2 minutes. Add the chicken stock and the caraway seeds. Simmer until the moisture from the sauerkraut is completely absorbed. Set the sauerkraut aside.

Melt the remaining 3 tablespoons of butter and brush both sides of the bread slices with it. Grill one side of the bread on on a griddle or in a wide sauté pan. Spread the ungrilled side of each bread slice with 1 tablespoon Russian dressing. Top with the duck meat and season with salt and pepper. Spread 1 tablespoon of cranberry sauce over the meat on each sandwich, and top with a slice of cheese. Melt the cheese under the broiler for 1 to 2 minutes, or until the cheese is hot and bubbly. Cut each sandwich into triangles and serve hot.

Makes 16 finger sandwiches.

Cabbage Stuffed with Pork and Veal

This traditional French country dish involves stuffing and braising a whole cabbage.

2 cups cubed sourdough
    bread
1 cup milk
½ pound ground pork
½ pound ground veal
2 cloves garlic, peeled and
    minced
¼ cup dried basil
2 eggs
1 large head green cabbage
¼ cup canola oil
3 cups peeled, diced carrots
1 medium onion, peeled
    and diced
About 2 cups homemade or
    canned chicken stock

Place the sourdough bread in a medium bowl and cover with the milk. Soak the bread until moist, 5 minutes or more. Gently squeeze the bread to remove any excess milk. In a large bowl, mix together the bread, ground pork, ground veal, garlic, and basil. Add the eggs and mix well. Set the stuffing mixture aside.

Trim the cabbage, removing any brown outer leaves, but leave it whole. Blanch the cabbage in a large pot of boiling salted water for 5 minutes. Remove the cabbage and invert to allow excess water to drain. Open the cabbage leaves until the head resembles a large flower. Beginning from the center, spread the stuffing mixture on the inside of the cabbage leaves. When the cabbage is completely stuffed, tie it securely with cotton string.

Heat the oil in a large, heavy saucepan with a lid. Add the carrots and brown until golden. Add the onion and cook over low heat until the onion is translucent. Place the stuffed cabbage on top of the carrots and onion, and cover. Braise the cabbage, adding small amounts of chicken stock as needed, for 2 hours. Cut the cabbage into wedges and serve with the carrots and onion.

Makes 6 servings.

Smoked Duck

We use a converted barrel drum for our grill, but you can use any covered grill. Follow the manufacturer's instructions if you use a commercial smoker.

1½ cups water
½ cup cranberry juice
½ cup soy sauce
¼ cup coarse or kosher salt
¼ cup honey
1 tablespoon minced onion
2 tablespoons grated fresh
   ginger
1 tablespoon dried
   rosemary, crumbled
1 large duck (4 to 5 pounds)
2 cups alder or other
   aromatic hardwood
   chips, soaked in water for
   ½ hour

Combine the water, cranberry juice, soy sauce, salt, honey, onion, ginger, and rosemary together in a large bowl. Taking care not to pierce the flesh, prick the duck skin with a sharp knife in several places. Marinate the duck in the mixture for 4 hours in a cool place, making sure the duck is submerged. Remove the duck and allow to air-dry for 30 minutes. Pat the bird completely dry with paper towels before smoking.

Prepare the grill, using either a covered kettle-style grill or an enclosed electric smoker with wire racks. If using a kettle-style grill, spread the bottom with coals and ignite. The coals are ready for the wood chips when covered with a light gray ash (about 30 minutes). Sprinkle the moistened wood chips over the coals. Set a drip pan half full of water above the coals. Place the duck on a rack above the drip pan. Cover the grill and smoke until the duck is cooked through, about 3 hours. Keep the wood chips moist, the coals burning, and the drip pan half full of water. Don't allow the fire to get too hot or to go below 170 degrees Fahrenheit. Cut duck into pieces and serve.

Makes 2 servings.

Braised Rabbit in Dark Beer

Serve this over a bowl of white rice and red beans, topped with bits of tomato and Monterey jack cheese.

7 tablespoons canola oil

2 large yellow onions, peeled and diced into ½-inch cubes

2 red bell peppers, cored, deveined, seeded, and diced into ½-inch cubes

3 tablespoons mild chili powder

2 tablespoons ground cumin

2 tablespoons dried oregano

1 teaspoon cayenne

2 teaspoons ground coriander

Salt and freshly ground pepper to taste

1½ cups (12 ounces) dark beer

1 cup homemade or canned chicken stock

1 tablespoon vinegar

1 rabbit (about 2½ pounds), cut up

Preheat the oven to 375 degrees Fahrenheit. In a large casserole, heat 4 tablespoons of the oil. Add the onions and sauté until softened, about 10 minutes. Add the peppers and sauté an additional 5 minutes. Stir in the chili powder, cumin, oregano, cayenne, and coriander. Season with salt and pepper to taste. Stir in the beer, chicken stock, and vinegar.

Heat remaining 3 tablespoons of oil in a large skillet. Sauté the rabbit on all sides until browned. Add the rabbit to the casserole, covering the meat with the sauce. Cover the casserole and place on the center rack of the oven. Bake until the rabbit is tender and thoroughly cooked, about 1 hour.

Makes 4 to 6 servings.

Riversong Lodge Fudge Brownies

We make brownies nearly every day at the lodge in the summer, then wrap them individually in plastic wrap and include them in river lunches. In the winter, our brownies sit on a large platter near the coffeepots.

1 cup unsalted butter

3 ounces unsweetened chocolate

3 cups sugar

5 eggs

1½ cups all-purpose flour

2 cups coarsely chopped pecans

2 ounces bittersweet chocolate, chopped

2 ounces milk chocolate, chopped

Preheat the oven to 350 degrees Fahrenheit. Grease and flour a 13-by-9-by-2-inch baking pan. Melt the butter and the unsweetened chocolate in a small, heavy-bottomed saucepan over low heat. Set aside.

Beat the sugar and eggs in a large mixer bowl on high speed for 10 minutes. Beat in the melted chocolate mixture on low speed. Add the flour, mixing just until blended. Add the nuts and the chopped chocolate, mixing well.

Pour the mixture into the prepared baking pan. Bake on the center rack of the oven until the center of the brownies is firm to the touch and a toothpick inserted comes out clean, about 35 to 40 minutes. Cool the brownies and cut into squares.

Makes 32 brownies.

Sourdough Starter

Sourdough is a subject of much intrigue and debate here in the North. For a true sourdough, you should rely on naturally occurring yeast and lactobacilli in your kitchen. For a quicker version of sourdough, add a packet of active dry yeast to the following recipe, but it won't be a true sourdough.

2 cups all-purpose flour
2 cups warm distilled water

Mix the two ingredients in a glass or ceramic bowl or a plastic pitcher. Cover with cheesecloth and let the mixture rest in a warm, draft-free place in the kitchen for 48 hours. The mixture should be the consistency of pancake batter, slightly bubbly, and sour smelling. Stir the mixture and store, covered, in the refrigerator.

See "Care and Feeding of a Sourdough Starter" on page 79 for information on how to keep a sourdough starter going.

Makes 2 cups sourdough starter.

Care and Feeding of a Sourdough Starter

Once you've made a sourdough starter, you can keep it going indefinitely. Some people have starters that have been handed down in their families like heirlooms. Follow these steps to keep your starter alive. I keep my starter in a 2-quart pitcher, but any covered glass, ceramic, or plastic container will work. Never use metal when working with yeast.

Store your starter in the refrigerator. To use the starter, remove as much from the container as you need and let it stand at room temperature until bubbly, about 1 hour. Replenish your starter by adding equal amounts of flour and water.

Feed your starter once every two weeks to a month. Do this by adding 1 cup each of flour and water to the starter. If you need a great deal of starter, increase its volume by adding up to 10 cups of flour per cup of starter and an equal amount of water. Let stand for 48 hours.

If a liquid forms on top of the sourdough, simply stir it back in. If the liquid becomes any color besides straw yellow, discard the sourdough.

Sourdough starter can be frozen for several months. The longer it is frozen, the more likely it is that changes will occur in bacterial cell structure. To use, remove the frozen sourdough from the freezer, thaw, replenish, and keep at room temperature for 24 hours.

See page 78 for Sourdough Starter recipe.

Spring

The Man on the Mountain

Finally we had made it through the darkest days of winter. Although snow was still deep on the ground, the February sunlight streamed through the lodge windows and gave us hope for spring. Carl had just finished the puzzle of laying the cottonwood flooring in the lodge. We sanded the floor time after time, then sealed it with layers of varnish. The boards had been drying around the wood stove of the small cabin where we had been living all winter, and it was good to get them down. We painted the pitcher pump near the sink a bright cherry red and hung a small crystal in the window that scattered light and color around the room. The lodge was taking form and becoming the quaint and comfortable place I had been picturing.

Near the front door of the lodge, we set up the citizen's band radio on the teak desk that was once in Carl's office in Anchorage. The desk would serve as a reception area for arriving guests. We attached the CB to a battery and hid the wires underneath the desk. From the radio came lively chatter through the day as distant neighbors talked to one another, mostly about the weather. The radio became background noise while we went about our chores.

Later that day, a conversation caught our attention. We could hear people talking between two airplanes flying near Denali (Mount McKinley). The airplanes were searching for a missing mountaineer, a Japanese climber named Naomi Uemura.

Uemura was attempting a solo winter ascent of Denali, something no one had ever completed successfully. He was a seasoned climber and adventurer, having already reached the summits of several mountains as well as conquering the North Pole by dog sled, among other feats. Uemura was a national hero in Japan.

Looking out at the mountain from our warm, safe cabin, we listened to the search intensify. As the days wore on, even the most optimistic of the searchers became skeptical regarding Uemura's survival. As concern for Uemura increased, so did my sense of sadness. He was possibly trapped in a crevasse and still alive, or in a snow cave somewhere, alive but too weak to move on. There was no way to help the man on the mountain.

I had never met Naomi Uemura, nor even seen a picture of him, yet I felt a tragic sense of human loss as I watched the mountain from my window. He would never know how many people, myself included, had been wishing him well, hoping for his safe return. His body was never recovered.

More than 75 people have died on Denali in the past 60 years, trying to achieve their personal dreams of reaching the mountain's summit. Hundreds of others have made it to the top and back, successfully pushing themselves to their limits.

For Uemura, Alaska meant a battle with a mountain. For me, it means creating a home on a river, with shiny wood floors and sparkling light streaming in through a window that looks out north to the mountain.

Morels Stuffed with Shrimp Mousse

I spent one wonderful afternoon with a woman named Margaret Leibenstein, who wrote a special book called *The Edible Mushroom.* On the deck of her lovely home in Cambridge, Massachusetts, we drank champagne and talked about food. This recipe is adapted from one of hers.

16 very large morels
10 medium shrimp, shelled
    and deveined
10 medium scallops, tough
    muscles removed
1 egg white, chilled
1 shallot, peeled and minced
Salt and freshly ground
    pepper to taste
¼ cup heavy cream, chilled
2 tablespoons unsalted
    butter, melted

Wash the morels to remove any grit. Cut the stems off at the base of the caps. Drain the morels on paper toweling.

Puree the seafood in a food processor. Chill thoroughly. Add the egg white and shallot to the seafood. Process until smooth and firm. Season with salt and pepper. Add the cream to the mixture, processing just until blended. Chill the seafood mixture for 15 to 30 minutes. The mixture should be firm enough to hold a shape.

Preheat the oven to 350 degrees Fahrenheit. Fill a pastry bag fitted with a straight tip with the seafood mixture. Fill the morels with the mixture.

Butter a small baking dish large enough to hold the morels. Stand the morels upright in the dish and drizzle the melted butter over the mushrooms. Set the filled casserole into a larger casserole. Add about 1 inch of hot water to the outer pan to make a hot water bath. Cover the mushrooms and bring the water to a boil. Transfer the two casseroles to the oven and bake for 20 minutes, basting once with the pan liquids. Serve the mushrooms warm.

Makes 4 servings.

Mushrooms in the Woods

In both spring and late summer, we have many mushrooms growing in the woods near the lodge. We are not always brave enough to eat our harvest, but it is always fun to find and try to identify them. Be sure to have any mushroom you pick identified by an expert before eating it.

Morels—I love to serve morels with a light cream sauce that adheres to the nooks and crannies of this mushroom's corrugated surface. We frequently stuff morels with various fillings as well.

Boletus edulis—The cap of the *Boletus edulis,* also called a cèpe or porcini, looks something like a hamburger bun. Underneath the cap, instead of gills, there is a spongy layer dotted with hundreds of tiny holes. This is our favorite mushroom. Sauté them in a little butter and toss them with fresh egg noodles for an exceptional meal.

Puffballs—My children love to hunt for mature puffballs and stomp on them to release their smoky cloud of spores. I look for immature ones that are completely white inside, with the consistency of cream cheese. Sauté puffballs with garlic and lemon. Their flavor is very subtle.

Shaggy manes—Don't drink alcohol with shaggy manes, because an allergic reaction can occur. These mushrooms look just like their name sounds. I like them best when they are young, served with eggs and Cheddar cheese on English muffins.

Hearty Halibut Chowder

Besides the salmon, trout, and pike that swim in our river, we have access to other Alaskan seafood, such as halibut. The shredded carrots and Cheddar cheese in this chowder make it distinctive.

3 tablespoons unsalted
  butter
1 large yellow onion, finely
  diced
2 large potatoes, scrubbed
  and diced (about 2 cups)
2 cloves garlic, peeled and
  minced
6 cups homemade or canned
  chicken stock
1 can (8 ounces) stewed
  tomatoes, diced
2 large carrots, peeled and
  shredded
Salt and freshly ground
  pepper to taste
1½ cups milk
½ cup heavy cream
2 pounds halibut fillets, cut
  into 1-inch cubes
½ cup shredded Cheddar
  cheese
Hot red pepper flakes to
  taste

Melt the butter in a large skillet. Add the onion and sauté until translucent, about 5 minutes. Add the potatoes and garlic. Cook, stirring well, until the potatoes are crisp-tender, about 7 minutes. Remove from heat.

Bring the chicken stock to a boil over high heat in a large saucepan. Reduce the heat and add the tomatoes, potato-onion mixture, and the carrots. Stir gently and simmer for 10 minutes. Check the stock for seasoning, adding salt and pepper if desired. Gradually stir in the milk, cream, and the halibut. Simmer, uncovered, for an additional 10 minutes. Reduce the heat to low and stir in the shredded cheese. Sprinkle the chowder lightly with the hot red pepper flakes. Serve immediately.

Makes 6 to 8 servings.

Roasted Whole Dolly Varden Stuffed with Herbs

Dolly Varden, also called arctic char, are related to trout and salmon. The fish have pink spots and are named after a Charles Dickens character who wore a pink-spotted dress. The term "whole-dressed fish" means that the fish has been gutted and scaled, with the gills removed but the head and tail left intact. "Pan-dressed" means that the head and tail have been removed.

Canola oil for brushing
2 1-pound whole-dressed
  Dolly Varden
Salt and freshly ground
  pepper to taste
About 10 herb sprigs, such
  as thyme or oregano
1 lemon, thinly sliced
¼ pound unsalted butter,
  melted

Preheat the oven to 450 degrees Fahrenheit. Lightly brush with oil a wire rack large enough to hold the fish. Set the rack on a baking sheet. Quickly rinse the fish under cold running water and pat dry with a paper towel. Season the cavity with salt and pepper and stuff with the herbs, reserving a few sprigs for garnish, and the lemon. Insert small wooden skewers through the edges of the fish cavity to secure it. Score the fish in several places with a small, sharp knife to ensure even cooking. Measure the thickness of the fish at the thickest part and note the measurement.

Place the fish on the oiled rack. Brush the fish with the melted butter. Roast until the flesh is opaque when cut into at the thickest part with a knife. It will take about 10 minutes per inch of thickness. Remove the fish from the oven to a serving platter and remove the skewers. Garnish with the reserved herb sprigs and serve immediately.

Makes 2 to 4 servings.

Crusty Baked Ham

Usually my girls don't care much for mustard, but they love this ham, sliced thin and served with mashed potatoes.

1 boneless smoked ham
  (about 5 pounds)
4 cups apple cider
1 cup Calvados or applejack
1 cup Dijon mustard
2 cups sourdough bread
  crumbs
½ cup light brown sugar
1 tablespoon apple cider
  vinegar

Place the ham in a deep, oven-proof casserole. Add the cider and Calvados. Cover and refrigerate overnight, turning the ham occasionally.

Remove the ham from the refrigerator and let it warm to room temperature. Preheat the oven to 350 degrees Fahrenheit. Remove the ham from the marinade, reserving the liquid, and pat dry. Spread the ham with the mustard, reserving 1 tablespoon. Mix the bread crumbs and brown sugar together. Roll the ham in the bread crumb mixture to coat thoroughly.

Put the ham in a roasting pan and bake 1 hour, or until golden and heated through. Let rest 15 minutes before serving. Meanwhile, place the reserved marinade in a small saucepan and boil over high heat until it is reduced by half. Whisk in the vinegar and the remaining 1 tablespoon mustard. Serve the sauce with the sliced ham.

Makes 6 to 8 servings.

Roast Leg of Lamb with Red Currant Glaze

Red currant jelly can be purchased in most stores. Serve this savory meat with steamed carrots tossed with dill and butter.

1 leg of lamb (about 6 pounds)
1 clove garlic, peeled and slivered
½ cup red currant jelly
1 tablespoon vinegar

Preheat the oven to 350 degrees Fahrenheit. Wipe the lamb with a damp cloth. Make small slits in the meat with a small, sharp knife, and insert the garlic slivers. Let the roast stand at room temperature for 30 minutes before cooking. Place a meat thermometer deep into the flesh of the lamb, not touching the bone. Then arrange the leg of lamb, fat side up, in an open pan on a rack and cook for 20 to 25 minutes per pound. The thermometer will register 130 for rare, 160 for medium, and 170 for well done.

The lamb will take about 3 hours to cook. About 15 minutes before removing from the oven, baste the lamb with a mixture of the red currant jelly and vinegar. Baste several times to form a glaze. Remove the lamb from the oven and carve into thin slices. Serve warm.

Makes 6 to 8 servings.

Leftover Spring Lamb Hash

This lunch dish is a perfect way to use leftover lamb. The combination of lamb, eggplant, garlic, and green pepper is delicious. I recommend using Thai jasmine rice, although more traditional Italian rice also works well.

2¼ cups water
2 tablespoons unsalted butter
2 teaspoons salt
1 cup white rice (preferably Thai jasmine)
1 cup diced eggplant
¼ cup olive oil
½ cup minced red onion
¼ cup diced green pepper
1 clove garlic, peeled and minced
1 can (20 ounces) stewed, diced tomatoes, drained
Salt and freshly ground pepper to taste
½ cup fresh basil, shredded (or 2½ tablespoons dried)
1½ cups diced cooked lamb
1 teaspoon grated lemon peel

Bring the water to a rapid boil. Add the butter and salt, and then add the rice. Reduce heat, cover, and simmer for 25 minutes or until the water is completely absorbed and the rice is tender.

While the rice is cooking, sauté the eggplant slowly in the olive oil until tender. Drain off any excess oil. Add the onion, green pepper, and garlic. Sauté until the onion is golden. Add the tomatoes. Season to taste with salt and pepper. Add the basil and lamb. Cover and simmer over medium heat until the basil is wilted and the lamb is warmed thoroughly, about 10 minutes.

Fluff the rice and stir in the lemon peel. Place the rice on individual plates or on a platter. Make a well in the center of the rice and fill with the lamb hash. Serve immediately.

Makes 4 servings.

Danish Pastry Cakes

These frosted sandwich cookies are nice to have at midday with a cup of coffee. Children love them.

PASTRY:
1 cup cold unsalted butter
2 cups all-purpose flour
¼ cup granulated sugar
1 egg yolk

FROSTING:
1 cup powdered sugar
1½ tablespoons unsalted
    butter, at room
    temperature
½ teaspoon minced orange
    peel
1 tablespoon orange juice

FILLING:
½ cup red raspberry
    preserves

Small orange wedges for
    garnish (optional)

To make the pastry, cut the butter into small pieces and rub into the flour. Add the sugar and egg yolk. Let the pastry rest for 1 hour, covered, in the refrigerator.

Preheat the oven to 350 degrees Fahrenheit. Grease a baking sheet. Roll the pastry out into two rectangles, each 9-by-12 inches. Cut each rectangle into about twelve 2-inch squares. (Be sure to cut an even number of squares.) Place the squares on the baking sheet. Bake on the center rack of the oven for 5 to 7 minutes or until a light golden color.

To make the frosting, beat the powdered sugar, butter, orange peel, and orange juice until fluffy.

To assemble the cakes, spread the frosting onto 12 of the pastry squares. Spread the filling onto the other 12 squares. Place one frosted pastry square on top of one pastry square with filling to form a small sandwich. Repeat with remaining squares. Decorate the tops with small wedges of fresh orange, if desired.

Makes about 12 small cakes.

Lemon Squares

We serve these tart squares on our deck as we watch the river flow by.

1 cup unsalted butter, at
room temperature
½ cup powdered sugar
2⅓ cups all-purpose flour
4 eggs
2 cups granulated sugar
1 teaspoon grated lemon
peel
¼ cup lemon juice
1 teaspoon baking powder
Powdered sugar, for dusting

Preheat the oven to 350 degrees Fahrenheit. Grease a 9-by-13-inch baking pan. In a large bowl, cream the butter and ½ cup powdered sugar until light and fluffy. Add 2 cups of the flour and beat until blended. Press the flour mixture into the prepared pan. Bake on the center rack of the oven for 20 minutes.

In a small bowl, beat the eggs and granulated sugar together until well blended. Add the lemon peel, lemon juice, remaining ⅓ cup flour, and baking powder. Beat until well blended. Pour the lemon mixture over the baked crust. Bake for 15 to 20 minutes, or until the lemon custard is golden and firm. Remove from the oven. Dust with powdered sugar. Cut into small squares after the pan has cooled.

Makes 16 squares.

Chocolate Ricotta Pie

Ricotta has become a staple in the Riversong pantry. It can be frozen for long periods with no change in consistency or flavor. This pie has a rich cheesy-chocolate flavor.

2 egg yolks
⅔ cup sugar
Peel of 1 lemon, finely
    minced
4 cups (2 pounds) ricotta
    cheese
2 ounces semisweet
    chocolate, chopped
Pastry for an 8-inch single-
    crust mealy pie shell
    (see "Two Kinds of Pie
    Crust," on pages 47
    and 48)

Preheat the oven to 350 degrees Fahrenheit. Beat the egg yolks with the sugar until creamy. Add the lemon peel. Beat in the ricotta and chocolate pieces.

Roll out the pastry and fit into an 8-inch pie pan, fluting the edges of the dough. Pour the ricotta mixture into the pie shell. Bake on the center rack of the oven for 1 hour, or until the pie is set and the top is golden brown.

Makes 6 to 8 servings.

Beer Pretzels

We have so many European guests at Riversong, it seemed natural to make pretzels for the bar. Half the fun is trying to relearn how to do that pretzel twist every time we make them. These pretzels are big and soft, and perfect for scooping up grainy European mustard.

Coarse or kosher salt
1 package (1 tablespoon)
   active dry yeast
2 tablespoons warm water
   (110 to 115 degrees
   Fahrenheit)
1⅓ cups light beer, at room
   temperature and flat
½ cup firmly packed light
   brown sugar
2 ounces unsweetened
   chocolate
3 cups all-purpose flour
Baking soda
Spicy, coarse-grained
   mustard, for dipping

Grease 2 baking sheets and sprinkle with coarse salt. Combine the yeast and 2 tablespoons warm water in a large mixing bowl. Stir until the yeast is dissolved. Add the beer and brown sugar and mix well.

Melt the chocolate over a double boiler. Cool to room temperature and stir into the yeast mixture. Add the flour to the yeast mixture, stirring until the dough no longer sticks to the bowl and is kneadable. Turn the dough out onto a floured surface and knead until it is smooth and elastic, about 10 minutes. Place the dough in a large, greased bowl, cover, and let rise in a warm place for 1 hour.

Punch down the dough and divide in half. Cover one half with plastic wrap and then work with the other half. Divide the dough into 8 pieces, each about the size of a golf ball (see drawings, page 96). Roll one piece back and forth into a long rope shape. (1) Form the rope into a U shape, and lay one end of the U over the other. (2) Twist the loop around once, then (3) fold the circular part of the pretzel down over the loop. Repeat with remaining dough. Let the pretzels rise, uncovered, on a floured baking sheet for 30 minutes.

continued on next page

Preheat the oven to 475 degrees Fahrenheit. Fill a large skillet with water, adding 1 tablespoon baking soda for each cup of water. Bring to a gentle boil over medium heat. Using a wide spatula, carefully lower a pretzel into the boiling water. Add additional pretzels, without overcrowding. Cook for 30 seconds. With a slotted spatula, transfer the pretzels to the prepared salted baking sheet. Repeat with the remaining pretzels. Sprinkle with coarse salt. Bake until the pretzels are firm, 8 to 10 minutes. Let cool slightly on a rack. Serve with a spicy, coarse-grained mustard.

Makes 16 pretzels.

1

2

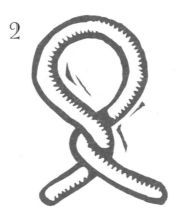

3

Spring Skiing

It was a glorious April day. The sky was clear blue, with not a cloud to be seen. I had planned to spend the morning in the greenhouse, starting tiny seedlings that would flourish and become small plants ready for the garden in June. I can spend hours in the greenhouse in spring. The heady mixture of warm, wet soil and sun streaming through the glass makes the atmosphere nearly tropical.

Carl built the greenhouse in 1988. He had to haul gravel up from the river in a wheelbarrow to mix concrete for the foundation. He dug eight feet into the earth to set the footers. We bought special thermo-insulated glass for the greenhouse that was so expensive and difficult to get to the lodge, we had to purchase and transport one panel of glass at a time.

Fifteen panels of glass later, the greenhouse is now a place I can't imagine living without. In the spring, we fill the glass room to the rafters with plant starts. After the first of June, the plants all go into the ground and the greenhouse is converted into a café-like setting with three small tables. In the winter, it is a perfect spot for viewing the northern lights. Like all things at Riversong, our glass room earns its keep.

This April day, Carl appeared at the door of the greenhouse and suggested that we make one final ski trip before the spring sun melted all the snow. I agreed to put aside my seed starting and take a trip up Lake Creek.

Along the river's edge, tiny streams of water were beginning to form and trickle toward the sea 100 miles away. Although nothing green was showing yet, I could imagine the fiddlehead ferns beginning to bud underneath the snow. Another few weeks and we would witness the phenomenon of the Alaskan breakup, when massive amounts of ice in the Yentna River wash out in one dramatic gush toward the sea.

We skied up to Bulchitna Lake, three miles north of the mouth of Lake Creek. It is part of a chain of lakes that once was home to a group of Alaska Natives, who called Bulchitna Lake *Bentalit*, "Where Lake Water Flows."

We skied out onto the frozen lake. The sun was warm on our faces, and the quietness of the place gave me an eerie feeling. I could imagine a Native village here, with women drying summer fish on racks and smoke rising from the fires. It must have been a harsh life for them, much harsher than my life now. No greenhouses for spring warmth and joy, no ski planes carrying supplies from town.

Once we reached the middle of the lake, we stopped to look around us. Only one sound broke the silence—the sound of cracking ice.

What would it be like if Carl and I fell into the lake? There was no one to see us or hear us. The spirits of ancient Indians would watch the scene without regard. The snow would keep melting, and the rivulets of water would keep trickling toward the sea.

We slowly made our way back to the edge of the lake, a little thrilled at the adventure, and a little humbled, too. For the next few weeks, we would confine ourselves to home, until the ice melted and the rivers flowed. Carl would put away the snowmobiles and skis and trade them for boats and oars. I would keep nurturing the seedlings in the green-house until the cold soil was warm enough to receive them in June.

Cranberry Crumble Muffins

These sweet and tart muffins have a nutty crumble topping. What could be better on a crisp Alaska morning?

MUFFINS:
½ cup unsalted butter
2 cups all-purpose flour
2 teaspoons baking powder
1 teaspoon baking soda
½ teaspoon salt
1 cup sugar
1 cup milk
2 large eggs
1 teaspoon vanilla extract
2 cups frozen cranberries,
    chopped and thawed

TOPPING:
½ cup sugar
½ cup all-purpose flour
¼ cup unsalted butter,
    chilled and cut into
    ¼–inch cubes
½ teaspoon ground
    cardamom
¼ cup ground walnuts

Preheat the oven to 375 degrees Fahrenheit. Grease 12 half-cup muffin tins. Set aside. Melt the ½ cup butter and cool to room temperature.

To make the muffins, combine the flour, baking powder, baking soda, salt, and sugar in a medium bowl. Combine the milk, melted butter, eggs, and vanilla in a second bowl, blending well. Combine the flour mixture and the egg mixture. Fill each muffin tin two-thirds full with the batter. Toss the cranberries in a small amount of flour to coat. Sprinkle some of the cranberries into each muffin tin.

To make the topping, combine the sugar, flour, butter, cardamom, and ground walnuts together, mixing until crumbly. Sprinkle the topping over the muffins.

Bake on the center rack of the oven for 15 to 20 minutes, or until a toothpick inserted in the center comes out clean.

Makes 12 muffins.

Honey Nut French Toast

When some of our French guests asked what we call this dish, they seemed delighted that it was known as French toast. Serve this French toast warm with Alaska birch syrup (see pages 256-57 for source list) and wild berry jams.

4 slices sourdough bread (cut 1 inch thick)
⅔ cup finely ground walnuts
4 large eggs
½ cup milk
1 teaspoon vanilla extract
⅓ cup Alaska fireweed, or other, honey
¼ cup unsalted butter

Trim the crusts from the bread. Use a food processor to chop the crusts into bread crumbs. Add the ground walnuts to the bread crumbs and set the mixture aside in a shallow dish.

Combine the eggs, milk, and vanilla in a shallow bowl. Make a slit to form a pocket into the side of each slice of bread. Spread a thin layer of honey into the pocket. Repeat with the remaining bread slices.

Dip each slice of bread into the milk mixture, then into the nut mixture, then again into the milk mixture. Melt the butter on a griddle or in a wide skillet over medium-high heat. Fry the bread for 2 to 3 minutes on each side, or until golden brown.

Makes 2 to 4 servings.

Blue Cheese Mousse with Port Sauce

Riversong chefs gather herbs fresh from the garden and prepare salmon that was swimming only minutes before. One talented chef offered this mousse as his specialty. It is a rich appetizer combining the sharp flavor of cheese with the sweetness and depth of port.

MOUSSE:

½ cup blue cheese

½ cup cream cheese

3 eggs

3 tablespoons heavy cream

1 tablespoon chopped fresh chives

Salt and freshly ground pepper to taste

Pinch of paprika

SAUCE:

2 cups heavy cream

¼ cup port

2 tablespoons homemade or canned chicken stock

1 tablespoon unsalted butter

9 ¼-inch-thick sourdough rounds, toasted

2 tablespoons chopped fresh herbs

2 tablespoons crumbled blue cheese

To make the mousse, preheat the oven to 350 degrees Fahrenheit. Butter nine 1½-ounce timbale molds. Soften and puree the blue cheese and cream cheese in a food processor. In a medium bowl, blend together the eggs, cream, chives, salt, pepper, and paprika. Add the egg mixture to the cheese and process until well blended, about 1 minute. Pour the mousse into the molds. Place the timbales in a baking pan. Add hot water to halfway up the sides of the timbales. Cover the timbales with buttered parchment paper. Bake for 30 minutes, or until the mousses are set.

To make the sauce, place the cream in a medium saucepan over medium-low heat. Boil until the cream is reduced to 1 cup. Add the port and the chicken stock. Continue to cook the sauce, stirring frequently, until it is thickened. Swirl in the butter and stir until melted.

To serve, top each sourdough round with a mousse. Nap with the sauce and garnish with fresh herbs and crumbled blue cheese. Serve warm.

Makes 9 servings.

Sweet Potatoes Anna

Potatoes Anna is a classic dish we have served at the lodge for years. It just seemed to make sense to try it with sweet potatoes.

½ cup clarified butter
4 medium sweet potatoes or yams (about 2½ pounds)
Salt and freshly ground white pepper to taste
½ cup shredded Parmesan cheese

Adjust the oven rack to its lowest position and preheat the oven to 425 degrees Fahrenheit. Line the bottom of a 9-inch round cake pan with a circle of aluminum foil and coat with 1 tablespoon of the clarified butter. Peel and slice the sweet potatoes into ⅛-inch rounds with a large knife or with a food processor fitted with a thin slicing disk.

Working in a spiral pattern, cover the bottom of the pan with a layer of closely overlapping sweet potato slices. Drizzle the potatoes with 1 tablespoon of the butter, and lightly sprinkle with salt, pepper, and 1 tablespoon of the cheese. Continue layering all of the potato slices in the same manner, using all of the melted butter and cheese. Cover the top of the potatoes with foil, pressing down firmly with your hands to compress the potatoes.

Bake the potatoes for 30 minutes. Remove the foil and bake until the potatoes are tender and the top is crisp and brown, 35 to 40 minutes longer. Cool the potatoes in the pan for 5 minutes. Run a sharp knife around the edge of the pan to loosen the potatoes. Carefully invert the potatoes onto a serving plate. Serve immediately.

Makes 6 servings.

Braised Veal with Cider and Oranges

I was a guest at the Veuve Clicquot champagne house in France, where I was treated to a lovely luncheon that included this dish. It was there that I tasted my first Rosé champagne. Serve the shanks with Robert Litti's Spaetzle (see page 241) or other hot, buttery noodles.

4 slices of veal shank (2 inches thick)

Salt and freshly ground pepper to taste

All-purpose flour

3 tablespoons olive oil

2 tablespoons unsalted butter

2 tablespoons minced shallot

1 head garlic, separated into cloves and peeled

1 large yellow onion, peeled and thinly sliced

½ cup tomato puree

1 cup homemade or canned beef stock

1 cup apple cider

2 sweet oranges, washed well

1 tablespoon cider vinegar

Preheat the oven to 375 degrees Fahrenheit. Season the veal with salt and pepper. Dredge the shanks in flour. Heat the oil and butter in a large, heavy, oven-proof casserole over medium-high heat. Brown the shanks on both sides. Remove the veal from the casserole and set aside. Add the shallot and garlic to the casserole. Sauté until the garlic has softened but not browned. Add the onion and sauté for 5 minutes, or until it has softened. Add the tomato puree, beef stock, apple cider, and cider vinegar. Bring the mixture to a simmer. Add the veal shanks. Cut the oranges into halves and arrange around the veal shanks. Cover and place the casserole in the oven. Braise for 1½ hours, or until the shanks are very tender. Serve warm.

Makes 4 servings.

Pan-roasted Spruce Grouse with Lemon and Herbs

At Riversong, spruce grouse, particularly hens, are favored at the lodge by European guests. The onion, lemon, and herbs in this recipe give the game bird a savory flavor. Substitute ptarmigan, partridge, or other grouse if you prefer.

4 large spruce grouse (about 1 pound each), rinsed thoroughly and patted dry

Salt and freshly ground pepper to taste

1 small onion, cut into wedges

1 small lemon, cut into wedges

¼ cup olive oil

2 tablespoons unsalted butter

1 tablespoon minced fresh tarragon, or 2 teaspoons dried tarragon

1 cup homemade or canned chicken stock

Preheat the oven to 400 degrees Fahrenheit. Season the birds inside and out with the salt and pepper. Place wedges of onion and lemon into the cavity of each bird. Tuck the wing tips underneath the birds, and truss them securely with cotton string.

Heat the olive oil and the butter in a large oven-proof skillet over medium heat until the butter mixture is hot but not brown. Put the birds in the skillet, breast side down. Sauté for 5 minutes, turning to lightly brown on all sides. Turn the birds breast side up. Add the tarragon and chicken stock to the pan. Cover the skillet with foil and place in the oven.

Roast until the juices of the thigh run pink, rather than red, when the thigh is pierced, about 35 minutes. Remove the birds from the skillet and cut in half. Discard the lemon and onion. Strain the pan juices and return to the skillet. Bring to a boil over medium-high heat and reduce the stock by half. Season to taste with salt and pepper. Place the birds on a warm serving platter and pour the stock over the birds. Serve immediately.

Makes 4 servings.

Glazed Corned Beef with Orange Horseradish Sauce

The sweetness of orange juice combined with the sharpness of lemon juice and chili powder make this dish intriguing. Corned beef is a favorite at the lodge.

3 pounds corned beef
1 cup light brown sugar
2 cups orange juice
1 tablespoon lemon juice
1 tablespoon English dry
   mustard
1 teaspoon chili powder
⅛ teaspoon cayenne
6 whole cloves
1 tablespoon grated fresh
   horseradish

Place the corned beef in a large pot and cover with boiling water. Bring to a gentle boil, reduce the heat, and simmer slowly for 3 hours, or until the beef is tender when pierced with a fork. (Corned beef shrinks if it is boiled too fast.) Remove the corned beef from the pot and set aside.

Preheat the oven to 375 degrees Fahrenheit. In a small saucepan, combine the brown sugar, orange and lemon juices, mustard, chili powder, and cayenne. Bring the marinade to a boil, reduce the heat, simmer for 5 minutes, and then set aside.

Insert the cloves on the fatty side of the beef, leaving two inches between them. Place the corned beef, fat side up, in a roasting pan large enough to hold it. Pour half the marinade over the corned beef and place the pan in the center of the oven. Roast the corned beef for 30 minutes, basting it with the marinade in the pan every 10 minutes. When the beef is glazed, remove it to a heated platter and cut it into thin slices.

Add the horseradish to the remaining marinade, heat it in a small saucepan over medium heat, and serve it with the corned beef slices.

Makes 6 to 8 servings.

Chocolate Potato Cake

This old-fashioned recipe uses leftover mashed potatoes. We serve this cake without frosting as a morning coffee cake, or drizzle it with a sugar frosting for dessert.

1 cup unsalted butter, at
    room temperature
2 cups sugar
1 teaspoon vanilla extract
1 teaspoon ground
    cinnamon
1 teaspoon ground nutmeg
2 cups cooked mashed
    potatoes, at room
    temperature
½ cup buttermilk
2¼ cups all-purpose flour
1½ teaspoons baking soda
½ cup unsweetened cocoa
    powder
4 eggs, well beaten
2 cups chopped walnuts

Preheat the oven to 325 degrees Fahrenheit. Grease a 10-inch tube pan. In a large bowl, cream the butter and sugar together. Add the vanilla extract and the spices. Mix well. Fold in the mashed potatoes. Add the buttermilk.

Sift together 2 cups of the flour, the baking soda, and the cocoa in a medium bowl. Add the flour mixture to the creamed mixture. Add the eggs.

Mix the remaining ¼ cup flour with the nuts. Add the nut mixture to the batter. Pour the batter into the tube pan and bake for 1 hour, or until a cake tester comes out clean. Remove from the oven and invert the cake onto a cooling rack before slicing.

Makes 8 to 12 servings.

Strawberry Jam Bars

Grating pastry dough into a baking pan is an unusual technique that I learned on a visit to England. I think it gives these strawberry-filled bars an interesting texture.

1 cup all-purpose flour
1 teaspoon baking powder
¼ teaspoon ground allspice
¼ teaspoon ground nutmeg
Pinch of salt
½ cup cold unsalted butter
¾ cup sugar
1 teaspoon honey
1 egg yolk
1 cup strawberry jam
½ cup finely chopped
  walnuts

Sift the flour, baking powder, allspice, nutmeg, and salt together. Cream the butter and sugar until light and fluffy, then beat in the honey and egg yolk. Add the flour mixture to the butter mixture and form into a dough. Wrap the dough in plastic wrap and chill for 1 hour.

Preheat oven to 350 degrees Fahrenheit. Grease an 8-by-8-by-2-inch pan. With a hand grater, coarsely grate half of the dough into the prepared pan. Press the dough down slightly with the palm of your hand. Spread the jam over the surface of the dough. Grate the other half of the dough over the jam. Sprinkle with the walnuts and press the dough lightly.

Place the pan in the center rack of the oven and bake for 30 minutes or until the pastry is golden in color. Cool in the pan, then slice into 2-by-4-inch bars.

Makes 8 bars.

Semifreddo

I learned to make a version of this classic Italian dessert from a wonderful man named Robert Cacciola. I cooked with him one evening at the James Beard House in New York City. The flavor of cranberries offers an Alaskan influence.

6 eggs, separated
⅔ cup sugar
¼ cup cranberry liqueur
2 cups heavy cream
Mint leaves for garnish

Line two standard loaf pans (5 by 9 by 3 inches) with heavy aluminum foil, so the foil overhangs the sides of the pan by several inches.

Beat the egg yolks with ⅓ cup of the sugar with an electric mixer or by hand until the yolks are light and fluffy, about 10 minutes. Place the yolks into the top of a double boiler over medium-low heat. Stir the yolk-sugar mixture constantly, adding the cranberry liqueur slowly, for 10 to 15 minutes, or until thick. Remove from heat and cool to room temperature.

Whip the cream, adding the remaining ⅓ cup sugar, until it forms stiff peaks. Refrigerate.

Beat the egg whites to stiff peaks. In a large bowl, fold one-third of the whipped cream into the egg yolk mixture. Fold in one-third of the egg whites and repeat the process, alternating between the whipped cream and the egg whites.

Place the mixture in the prepared pans and cover with the overhanging aluminum foil. Place in the freezer for 8 to 10 hours before serving.

Remove the semifreddo from the pans, inverting it onto a platter. Peel off the aluminum foil, then slice into 1½-inch wedges. Serve drizzled with additional cranberry liqueur and garnished with mint leaves.

Makes 12 servings.

The Bear Fair

When our oldest daughter was ready to start school, we signed her up with the correspondence program offered by the state of Alaska. We decided to school her at home in the spring and summer, and then take a break in the wintertime to coincide with our lodge schedule. The school-by-mail program offers children throughout rural Alaska a fine education, whether they are on a fishing boat in the Pacific Ocean or in a fishing lodge on the Yentna River.

The day her first big box of books and supplies arrived at Riversong, Carly, the new kindergartner, became so excited that her chest broke out in a rash. We unpacked the mysterious world of school onto our living room floor: pencils, paper, colorful workbooks, audiotapes, and books. It was as if everything new and exciting in the world came spilling out of that box.

One of Carly's first school days involved creating a fantasy event called a bear fair. She spent the day gathering her favorite stuffed animals, including a few reluctant real animals, such as Jim the cat. Along with her sister, Amanda, the group assembled in the living room underneath the large picture window that overlooks the river.

I was busy about my chores, carrying in a basket of laundry from outside. Entering the cabin from the back door, I listened to the pleasant sounds of the girls playing. Suddenly, something made me look up. A huge black bear was stretched across the window, staring inquisitively at the scene inside. I dropped my basket and probably let out some kind of yell, telling the girls to move away. I feared that the weight of the bear would break the window and that he would come crashing in on the children. When I rushed toward Carly and Amanda, the bear let out a roar and ran away. The girls regarded the whole episode as a mere distraction and returned to their game. I'll bet Carly was the only kindergartner who had a real bear come to her bear fair.

Earlier that year, we had experienced another bear incident. A white Chinese goose had been sitting on her huge nest of eggs for nearly three weeks. She was so diligent; she wouldn't budge from her nest. The eggs must have been ready to hatch soon. We would bring her food and water, and we all fretted about her condition as part of our daily conversation.

One afternoon, a huge black bear, maybe the same one that visited the bear fair, found her nest, abruptly pushed her off, and sat down next to the nest like a small child playing. He popped the eggs into his mouth, one after the other, until all 21 were gone. The mother goose squawked loudly and we tried to shoo the bear away, but he was too involved in his egg feast. Even shots sent deliberately over his head from Carl's shotgun didn't break his concentration. When the bear was finished, he slowly made his way into the woods. We felt sad, not for the loss of our imminent gosling flock, but for the dutiful mother who had been so true to her nest.

We hardly ever eat bear meat at Riversong. It has a strong flavor that few appreciate, and outside of really well barbecued bear ribs, we relegate bear meat to homemade dog food. But bear time at the lodge usually means that berry time is not far away, and berries have a wild flavor everyone enjoys.

Macaroni and Cheese

We love to make macaroni and cheese in many variations. It is nearly a universal food. This white and green version combines Greek olives, feta cheese, sour cream, salsa, and spinach.

1 onion, finely chopped
¼ cup unsalted butter
1 pound elbow macaroni
1 cup sour cream
½ cup crumbled feta cheese
¼ cup sliced Greek olives
    (about 15 olives)
Salt and freshly ground
    pepper to taste
1 cup spinach, cooked,
    drained, and chopped
½ cup chunky mild tomato
    salsa
½ cup shredded Parmesan
    cheese (optional)

In a skillet, sauté the onion in the butter until it is soft and golden. Cook the macaroni in boiling salted water until tender. Drain.

In a bowl, mix the hot macaroni, onion, sour cream, feta, and olives. Toss well and season to taste with salt and pepper. Add the spinach and toss again. Stir in the mild salsa. Sprinkle with Parmesan cheese, if desired. Serve warm.

Makes 6 to 8 servings.

Egg and Bacon Breakfast Pizza

Breakfast pizza toppings can be mixtures of all kinds: jam and fruit, red flannel hash with a poached egg, or smoked salmon mixed with scrambled eggs. There are wonderful commercial pizza crusts available if you don't want to make your own.

8 large eggs
4 teaspoons heavy cream
4 teaspoons unsalted butter
Salt and freshly ground
   pepper to taste
4 small pizza crusts,
   (6 inches diameter),
   prebaked
8 bacon strips, cooked
½ cup shredded Parmesan
   cheese
4 tablespoons shredded basil
Spicy salsa, as an
   accompaniment

Preheat the oven to 350 degrees Fahrenheit. Gently beat the eggs with the cream. Melt the butter in a sauté pan over medium heat. Add the egg mixture, lightly scramble the eggs, and season with salt and pepper to taste.

Divide the eggs into 4 equal portions and place on the prebaked pizza crusts. Crumble the bacon and sprinkle it over the eggs. Sprinkle the Parmesan cheese and basil equally over each pizza. Place the pizzas onto a baking sheet and bake for 1 to 2 minutes, or until the cheese is melted. Serve with a spicy salsa.

Makes 4 servings.

Frikadeller Soup

It continues to be a challenge to prepare foods that my young daughters truly relish. They love to help me make this Danish soup. Frikadeller are small Danish meatballs usually made from pork. I prefer to make them with lean beef.

1 pound lean ground beef
1 small red onion, finely chopped
2 tablespoons coarsely chopped pine nuts
¼ cup cooked brown rice, cooled
½ cup shredded carrot
1 egg, beaten
Salt and freshly ground pepper to taste
Canola oil, for frying
8 cups homemade or canned beef stock
2 tablespoons tomato paste
2 medium potatoes, washed and cubed
1 tablespoon dried basil

In a large bowl, combine the ground beef, onion, pine nuts, rice, carrot, and egg. Season with salt and pepper. Shape the mixture into small balls. Wet your hands with cold water, if necessary, to make the shaping easier.

Add enough oil to a large skillet to lightly coat the bottom. Heat the skillet over medium-high heat. Add enough of the meatballs to fit in the pan without crowding. Brown well on all sides. Remove the meatballs with a slotted spoon and continue with the next batch until all the meatballs are browned.

Bring the beef stock to a boil in a large, heavy saucepan. Stir in the tomato paste. Add the potatoes and return to a boil. Reduce heat and simmer for 10 minutes.

Add the meatballs to the broth. Simmer for 20 minutes or until the meatballs are firm and the potatoes are tender. Serve in warmed bowls, sprinkled with basil.

Makes 4 servings.

Pasta with Halibut, Swiss Chard, Rhubarb, and Bacon

At Riversong, rhubarb is the first green thing to push up through the snow in the spring. Our rhubarb plants supply us all spring and summer. This dish combines the rich, buttery flavor of halibut with the sharp contrast of Swiss chard, rhubarb, and crisp bacon.

6 slices bacon

8 ounces dried fettuccine

½ cup fine sourdough bread crumbs

2 large cloves garlic, peeled and minced

1 pound (about 3 cups) Swiss chard, deribbed and chopped

1 cup rhubarb, cut into ¼-inch dice

1 pound halibut, broiled and flaked

½ teaspoon hot red pepper flakes

Salt and freshly ground pepper to taste

Fry the bacon until crisp and brown over medium heat in a medium sauté pan. Remove from the pan and drain on paper toweling. Reserve the bacon grease.

Bring 4 quarts salted water to a boil. Add the fettuccine to the water and cook until tender, about 10 minutes. Drain and rinse. Set aside.

In the same medium sauté pan, heat 3 tablespoons of the reserved bacon grease. Add the bread crumbs and garlic. Sauté until the bread crumbs are golden brown. Remove the bread crumb mixture from the pan and set aside.

Add the remaining bacon grease to the pan (about 2 tablespoons). Add the Swiss chard and the rhubarb. Sauté for 5 minutes or until the chard is wilted and the rhubarb is soft. Add the halibut and heat thoroughly. Add the bacon and bread crumbs. Combine the halibut mixture with the pasta. Return the pasta to the sauté pan and heat thoroughly, adding a little butter or olive oil if necessary. Sprinkle in the hot pepper flakes. Season to taste with salt and pepper, and serve warm.

Makes 4 servings.

Chicken-Apple Sausages

We love these sausages for breakfast. Use the same technique for a variety of fillings—caribou and cranberries, moose meat and onions, turkey and corn bread. The sausage can be stuffed into casings or formed into patties and sautéed.

½ pound pork fat

3 medium onions, chopped coarsely

3 medium tart green apples (such as Granny Smith), peeled, cored, and diced

¾ cup fine dry bread crumbs

½ cup milk

6 cloves garlic, peeled and minced

2 pounds boneless, skinless chicken breast, diced

2½ teaspoons salt

2 eggs

2 egg whites

½ cup heavy cream

Salt and freshly ground white pepper to taste

Sausage casing for 3 pounds of filling (optional, see note)

Butter for frying

Process the pork fat in a food processor until finely chopped. Put half of the fat into a large skillet and cook until it is melted and slightly brown. Add the onions and apples, stirring until the onions are translucent and golden, about 15 minutes. Place the remaining fat in the food processor. Add the bread crumbs, milk, garlic, and the sautéed onion and apple mixture. Process until the mixture is pureed. Remove the mixture to a bowl.

In the food processor, puree the chicken with the salt, eggs, egg whites, and cream. Combine the chicken and the apple-onion mixture, mixing well. Add salt and pepper to taste.

To stuff the sausage into casings, fit a pastry bag with a ½-inch tip. Fill the pastry bag two-thirds full with the chicken-apple mixture. Prepare the casing as indicated in the note below. Fill the casing with the chicken-apple mixture, twisting the casing at 6-inch intervals. Twist the end of the casing to close. If air bubbles form, prick them with a pin. If the casing tears, just remove the filling and tie it off.

Bring 6 quarts of water to a boil in a large kettle. Add the sausage links and immediately turn off the stove. Cover the kettle and let the

continued on next page

sausages stand until they are firm, about 30 minutes. Remove the sausage links, drain, and cut apart.

If you prefer, you can form the sausage meat into patties rather than using casings. Over medium heat, melt enough butter to coat the bottom of a 12-inch skillet. Add the sausages or patties to the skillet and brown on all sides.

A note on casings: Sausage casing can usually be purchased from good meat markets. It may come in one long piece, which you should cut into workable lengths, several yards per segment. Rinse the casing well with cool water before filling. Keep the casing in cool water while you prepare the sausage mixture. Drain and squeeze the casing gently.

Makes 3 pounds.

Honey Orange Cheesecake with Walnut Crust

This dessert is an elegant completion for any summer meal. Press the ground walnuts into the cheesecake after it is baked to form the walnut crust.

¼ cup sugar

1 pound cream cheese, softened

½ cup honey

6 egg yolks

1½ tablespoons grated orange peel

1½ teaspoons vanilla extract

3 cups sour cream

1 cup finely ground walnuts

Preheat the oven to 350 degrees Fahrenheit. Prepare an 8-by-2-inch springform pan by greasing the pan well. Add parchment paper to the bottom of the pan and cover the outside with heavy aluminum foil to prevent any water seepage.

In a large bowl, beat the sugar, cream cheese, and honey until smooth. Add the egg yolks, one at a time, beating until the batter is smooth. Add the grated peel, vanilla, and sour cream, and mix until blended.

Pour the batter into the prepared pan. Place the cheesecake into a large roasting pan filled with 1 inch of hot water. Bake the cheesecake on the center rack of the oven for 45 minutes.

Turn off the oven and let the cake set in the oven for an hour. Remove the cheesecake from the roasting pan, cool to room temperature, cover with plastic wrap, and refrigerate overnight.

Carefully remove the cheesecake from the springform pan, inverting it first onto a plate, then reinverting it onto a serving platter. Press the walnuts onto the sides and top of the cake.

Makes 10 to 12 servings.

Honey Love

Alaska produces some of the finest honey in the world. Bees are easy to keep, and one hive can produce up to 50 pounds of honey per year. Fireweed honey is the most common type of honey produced in Alaska.

Try making a honey-pepper marinade by adding 1½ teaspoons of hot red pepper flakes to 1 pound of honey. Cook the mixture over low heat for 10 minutes. Let stand for 1 hour. Strain and pour the honey into a jar with a lid. Before broiling, baste chicken or game with this marinade.

Use honey when baking quick breads to keep them moist longer. To change a recipe that calls for sugar, substitute honey for half of the sugar. Reduce the amount of liquid in the recipe by ¼ cup, and add ½ teaspoon of baking soda. Reduce the oven temperature by 25 degrees Fahrenheit to keep the honey from burning.

To make honey-nut brittle, combine 2 cups of honey with ½ cup of water and bring to a boil. Add 1 cup butter. Stir the mixture until it reaches the soft-ball stage. Add 2 cups of chopped nuts and spread the mixture onto a well-greased baking sheet. When the brittle has cooled, loosen it from the pan and break into pieces.

Make a tart lemonade, using only as much sugar as necessary. Dip the rims of margarita glasses in honey, then in coarsely granulated sugar. Freeze the glasses and serve with the lemonade and crushed ice.

Homemade Marshmallows

This recipe came from a magazine called *The Pleasures of Cooking*. Once our children had tried these, they never viewed store-bought marshmallows with any regard.

¼ cup powdered sugar
¼ cup cornstarch
1 cup granulated sugar
2 tablespoons light corn
   syrup
⅔ cup water
⅓ ounce unflavored gelatin
   (1½ envelopes)
¼ cup cold water
3 large egg whites
¼ teaspoon vanilla extract

Lightly butter a 9-by-9-by-2-inch pan. Sift together the powdered sugar and cornstarch. Use about 1 tablespoon of this mixture to coat the pan and reserve the remainder. Place the granulated sugar, corn syrup, and ⅔ cup water in a 1½-quart saucepan, and bring to a boil over medium-high heat, cooking until it reaches the soft-ball stage (250 degrees Fahrenheit), about 10 minutes.

In a 1-quart saucepan, heat the gelatin and ¼ cup cold water over low heat until the gelatin is dissolved. Keep warm until needed. With an electric mixer, beat the egg whites until they form stiff peaks. Continue to beat while slowly adding the hot sugar syrup. Add the gelatin mixture, then add the vanilla and continue to beat until the egg whites are cool, about 10 minutes. Pour the mixture immediately into the prepared pan and smooth the surface. Let stand in a cool, dry place for 2 hours.

Remove the marshmallow from the pan, using a sharp knife to loosen the edges. Dust with the remaining sugar-cornstarch mixture. With a sharp knife, cut into 1-inch squares. Dry the squares on a wire rack for 1 hour. Cover the marshmallows and store in a cool, dry place. They will last for 3 to 4 weeks.

Makes 81 marshmallows.

Swimming Salmon Tortilla Chips

Everyone enjoys these deep-fried chips, which we serve at the bar.

6 to 8 fresh corn tortillas
(a mixture of yellow and
blue looks great)
Canola oil for deep frying
Salsa for dipping

Stack the tortillas on a plate. Cover with a lightly dampened dish towel, and wrap the entire stack in plastic wrap to prevent it from drying out while you are working. Remove a tortilla from the stack and place it on a cutting board. Using a cookie cutter in the shape of a small salmon (or a template that you draw yourself), cut the tortilla into fish shapes. Cut each shape close to the last one to get as many salmon as possible from each tortilla. After the shapes are cut out, deep-fry them and serve warm with salsa for dipping.

Makes 24 to 30 chips.

Honey Apple Rolls

These rolls are scrumptious for breakfast, slathered with butter and a little whipped honey. The blend of sharp cheese with sweet apples is a favorite at the lodge.

8 cups all-purpose flour
1 tablespoon salt
1 cup honey
3 cups warm water (110 to 115 degrees Fahrenheit)
1½ packages (1½ tablespoons) active dry yeast
½ cup shredded apple
1 cup shredded sharp Cheddar cheese
¼ cup finely chopped walnuts
1 egg

Combine 4 cups of the flour and the salt in a medium bowl. In a large bowl, add the honey and warm water to the yeast and stir until smooth. Add the flour mixture to the yeast. Gradually stir in enough of the remaining flour to make a soft dough. Knead the dough on a floured surface for 10 minutes, until smooth. Transfer the dough to a bowl and let rise in a warm place until doubled in bulk, about 45 minutes.

Combine the apple, cheese, and walnuts in a medium bowl. Punch the dough down and cut into 24 equal pieces. Place a little bit of the apple-cheese mixture into the center of each piece of dough and shape into a round roll. Make sure the apple-cheese mixture is well encased in dough. Place the rolls about 2 inches apart on a well-greased baking sheet. Let rise again until doubled in bulk, about 45 minutes.

Preheat the oven to 350 degrees Fahrenheit. Lightly beat the egg in a small bowl. Brush each roll with a little of the beaten egg. Bake until the rolls are golden brown, about 15 to 20 minutes.

Makes 24 rolls.

Sweet Potato Baskets

These deep-fried baskets can be filled with many different fillings. My children love them, filled with anything from salads or fruits to main courses. Try them with bacon and scrambled eggs for breakfast, fresh seafood salad at lunch, or even honey-roasted nuts on the hors d'oeuvres tray. White potatoes work well in place of the sweet potatoes.

*1 pound sweet potatoes,
    peeled and shredded*
2 tablespoons cornstarch
*Salt and freshly ground
    pepper to taste*
Canola oil for deep frying

Mix the sweet potatoes, cornstarch, and salt and pepper. You'll need 2 metal strainers, one smaller than the other, to shape the "basket." In a large saucepan, heat enough oil to submerge the strainers. Dip the strainers into the oil to grease them.

Press a layer of the sweet potato mixture into the larger strainer. Put the smaller strainer into the larger one, sandwiching the mixture between the two strainers. Carefully dip the strainers into the hot oil, using a glove or hot pad in case the handles get too hot to touch.

After 3 minutes, remove the smaller basket and continue to fry for 10 minutes, or until the basket is crisp and golden. Remove the potato basket from the strainer and drain on paper towels. Repeat with remaining sweet potato mixture.

Makes 2 or 3 baskets, depending on size.

Twelve Eggs for an Angel Food Cake

One of the great pleasures in the Riversong kitchen is the spontaneity we enjoy in our creativity. We devise a weekly menu but often make changes at the last minute. A freshly found crop of currants leads to an impromptu pie. Gathered herbs perk up a vinaigrette for a just-picked salad. A visit to the chicken coop yields eggs for the morning omelet.

Walking out to the coop and gathering eggs is a chore that not everyone around the lodge loves. It's one that I particularly appreciate because we used to let our chickens run free so they could forage in the wooded area surrounding the lodge. Now we have them penned in a comfortable, well-fenced area behind the kitchen. We enjoyed the idea of free-ranging chickens, and they were probably very healthy, but I could never find their eggs.

I don't remember who told me that chickens are dumb, but I don't believe it. They are masters of disguise and intrigue. Hunting down the popular egg-laying spot of the day of our free-ranging chickens was a challenge for the best of sleuths. I was fascinated that our chickens laid eggs together in a communal nest, and that the location of the nest changed as often as I could find it. Which chicken was the nest scout? I never saw our whole flock of 30 chickens march off into the woods together on a laying expedition. How did they pass the message on to one another?

There were some close calls when the success of a meal depended on my ability to find chicken eggs hidden in the yard. One time I decided that I would make an angel food cake for dessert and serve it with fresh berries. It was about 4:30, which was a little late for me to be deciding what to make. I went off on a wild search through the woods to find the 12 eggs I needed. I couldn't find even one.

I searched out where large fallen logs were nearly hidden by the tall grass. There were a few rotten tree stumps that seemed to be nest favorites, near the currant shrubs. I looked under the pile of firewood near the Caribou Cabin, even down the trail to the west where the chickens sometimes went to lay eggs. I was beginning to think about other options for dessert—maybe poached pears in wine or a simple cheese platter served with port. Heading back to the house with my empty willow basket, I nearly stepped on a poor startled hen. She ran away from me, zigzagging through the tall grass as fast as she could go, announcing my presence to all the other chickens that were somewhere in the trenches. I looked down, and there was a nest—with exactly 12 eggs!

Now our chickens are much more civilized, living in their penned area. I don't necessarily miss those moments of panic, but I feel a small sense of loss without the hunt. I miss that feeling of childlike delight as I dug through the bushes to find a nest brimming with cleverly hidden, freshly laid eggs.

Shrimp and Crab Cakes

Shrimp and crab are available fresh in Alaska all year round because our coastline is so expansive. I prefer spot shrimp and Dungeness crabs for this appetizer dish. Serve the cakes with a favorite dipping sauce—sweet, savory, or spicy.

*1 pound raw shrimp, peeled
  and deveined*
1 egg
1 cup heavy cream
*Salt and freshly ground
  pepper to taste*
*1 pound flaked, cooked
  crabmeat*
½ cup fine dry bread crumbs
*¼ cup finely minced red
  onion*
1 tablespoon Dijon mustard
*¼ teaspoon hot red pepper
  sauce*
½ cup canola oil, for frying

In a food processor, puree the shrimp, egg, cream, salt, and pepper. Transfer the mixture to a medium bowl. Add the crabmeat, bread crumbs, onion, mustard, and red pepper sauce. Blend well. Shape the mixture into 2-inch patties, about ¼ inch thick.

Pour enough canola oil into a skillet to cover the bottom of the pan. Place enough of the cakes into the skillet to fit comfortably without crowding. Sauté the cakes over medium-high heat until one side is crisp and golden, about 7 minutes. Turn the cakes over and sauté on the other side. Drain on paper toweling. Repeat with remaining cakes, and serve warm.

Makes 36 2-inch cakes.

Baked Eggs with Basil

I prepare baked eggs many different ways—with meats, cheeses, or sauces. The combination of eggs, cream, and basil has always appealed to me. My favorite is eggs with purple basil, although this herb is difficult to grow at Riversong. If you don't have individual custard cups, you can bake the eggs together in a well-greased baking pan.

2 tablespoons unsalted butter
½ cup heavy cream
2 tablespoons dried basil, or 3 tablespoons chopped fresh basil
4 eggs
Freshly ground pepper to taste
6 tablespoons shredded Swiss cheese

Preheat the oven to 400 degrees Fahrenheit. Butter four 4-ounce custard cups. Into each cup pour 1 tablespoon of the cream and stir in 1 teaspoon of the basil. Break 1 egg into each custard cup and pour 1 tablespoon of the cream over it. Sprinkle the eggs with the remaining basil, a grind of pepper, and the cheese.

Place the custard cups into a baking pan and pour boiling water into the pan to come one-third of the way up the sides of the custard cups. Bake until the eggs are medium soft, about 7 minutes. Serve warm.

Makes 4 servings.

Egg Salad Sandwiches

We make mayonnaise every day with our own chicken eggs. In the spring, we can use our food processor because the generator is running, but in the winter we make it by hand. We use smoked salmon and a wonderful Russian dressing to make this egg salad unusual.

RUSSIAN DRESSING:
1 pint mayonnaise
1 teaspoon minced cooked
  beets
1 teaspoon minced red bell
  pepper
1 teaspoon minced green
  bell pepper
1 teaspoon minced Italian
  flat-leaf parsley
1 teaspoon minced chives
1 teaspoon caviar

EGG SALAD:
8 hard-cooked eggs

8 sourdough rye toast points
8 small slices cold-smoked
  salmon

To make the dressing, combine the mayonnaise, beets, red and green pepper, parsley, chives, and caviar. Add more of any one ingredient to taste, if desired.

To make the egg salad, peel and coarsely chop the eggs and place in a bowl. Add enough Russian dressing to just coat the eggs, reserving the remainder for another use. Serve on sourdough rye toast points with a sliver of smoked salmon on top.

Makes 8 sandwiches.

Alaska Cobb Salad

We're allowed to reinvent classics here in the Far North. Smoked halibut, not traditionally found in a Cobb salad, is available by mail order (see "Alaska Source List" in the back of the book), and it's worth sending away for. I like to serve this salad with a blue cheese dressing, but oil and vinegar can be good, too. Serve the salad with walnut bread and whipped honey butter.

1 medium head iceberg
    lettuce, finely shredded
2 cups mixed salad greens,
    such as leaf lettuce, cress,
    and arugula
1½ pounds smoked halibut,
    flaked
6 hard-cooked eggs, peeled
    and coarsely chopped
10 slices bacon, cooked until
    crisp, crumbled
6 ounces Danish blue cheese,
    or other blue cheese,
    crumbled
½ cup dried currants
1 red onion, peeled and
    sliced into thin rings
2 large tomatoes, cut into
    wedges
Salad dressing of your choice

In a large bowl, toss the greens. Add the halibut, eggs, bacon, cheese, currants, onion, and tomatoes, tossing lightly. Serve with the salad dressing on the side.

Makes 6 servings.

Fresh Egg Pasta

We use this master recipe for many different pasta dishes. We like to use our own chicken eggs for the rich color of the yolks. Add beet juice for pink pasta, unsweetened chocolate for dark pasta, or chopped peppers for spicy pasta.

2 cups all-purpose flour
3 eggs, lightly beaten
1 tablespoon canola oil
1 teaspoon salt

Mound the flour onto a clean work surface and make a well in the center. Add the eggs, oil, and salt to the well. Use your fingers to mix the flour in from the sides. Knead the dough until it is smooth and elastic, about 10 minutes. Cover the dough and let it rest for 30 minutes before rolling it out.

Roll the dough and cut into ¼-inch strips, either by hand or with a pasta machine. Drop the noodles into 4 quarts of boiling salted water and cook until al dente, about 3 to 5 minutes.

Makes 1 pound.

The Wild Harvest

Fireweed—Fireweed is a tall plant that produces spikes of pretty pinkish purple flowers. It grows wild all over Alaska. We serve the young shoots in salads in the spring and use the flowers tossed over salmon. The purple and coral combination is stunning.

Strawberry blite—This little plant, also called strawberry spinach or goosefoot, has mild leaves and clumps of tiny red berries that taste faintly of strawberry. We serve leaves as a green and the fruit as a garnish. It has a high vitamin C content.

Chickweed—Chickweed came to our garden as weed seed on the bottom of someone's shoes. It wasn't growing wild when we first arrived at Riversong. I learned that chickweed is a popular green in Europe and have been throwing it into salads ever since.

Fiddleheads—Although all ferns produce fiddleheads, or tightly curled shoots, only ostrich fern fiddleheads are edible. We gather fiddleheads in the spring along the banks of Lake Creek just north of the lodge, and serve them sautéed with lemon and butter.

Wild roses—Wild roses grow all over our yard. In the spring and summer, we use the petals in rose petal jelly and syrups, and as a garnish. In the fall, we eat rose hips in jams, sauces, and butter. My daughters make a paste of rose petals, then roll the paste into beads, prick the beads with pins, and let them dry in the greenhouse. Then they string the beads onto dental floss to make lovely necklaces.

Smoked Salmon Omelet in a Basket

This makes an unusual breakfast or brunch dish, with its combination of cashews and salmon. You can make the baskets the day before, then reheat them briefly in the oven.

2 tablespoons canola oil
1 onion, peeled and minced
2 stalks celery, minced
½ cup minced red bell
  pepper
½ cup minced wild
  mushrooms
Salt and freshly ground
  pepper to taste
6 eggs, beaten
1 pound kippered salmon,
  cut into strips
6 small Sweet Potato
  Baskets (see page 122)
3 green onions, minced
¼ cup chopped cashews

Heat the oil in a large skillet. Sauté the onion, celery, and pepper until softened, about 5 minutes. Add the mushrooms and season with salt and pepper to taste. Add the eggs, cook until set, and flip the omelet. The omelet should be very firm. Remove the omelet from the pan and cut into ¼-inch strips.

Divide the omelet strips and the salmon strips equally among the Sweet Potato Baskets. Sprinkle with green onions and cashews. Serve warm.

Makes 4 to 6 servings.

Russian Salmon Pie

Historically, Russians used the spinal cords of sturgeons to thicken this pie. This version is my adaptation, as most traditional recipes don't call for brown rice or cabbage.

3 tablespoons unsalted butter
1 onion, peeled and sliced into thin rings
½ pound domestic mushrooms, sliced
½ head green cabbage, shredded
2 sheets frozen puff pastry, thawed
1½ pounds Alaska salmon, cooked and flaked
2 cups cooked brown rice
½ cup shredded Cheddar cheese
½ cup fine bread crumbs
Salt and freshly ground pepper to taste
2 tablespoons minced fresh dill
1 hard-cooked egg, chopped
¼ cup heavy cream
1 egg, beaten

Preheat the oven to 375 degrees Fahrenheit. Melt the butter in a wide sauté pan over medium heat. Add the onion and sauté until softened, about 5 minutes. Remove from the pan and set aside. In the same pan, sauté the mushrooms and cabbage until the cabbage is wilted, about 5 to 7 minutes, adding butter if necessary. Set aside.

Take one sheet of the puff pastry and roll it out into a 12-by-12-inch square on a lightly floured surface. Place it in a 10-inch deep-dish pie pan, leaving the excess dough draped over the sides. Sprinkle the cooked salmon evenly over the bottom of the pastry, then top with the cooked brown rice and the shredded cheese.

Mix together the onion, mushrooms, cabbage, and bread crumbs. Season with salt and pepper. Spread this mixture over the cheese. Add the dill and egg. Pour the cream over the cabbage.

Roll out the remaining puff pastry on a lightly floured surface. Brush the rim of the pie with a little water. Place the pastry over the top of the pie. Cut small slits in the pastry to let the steam escape, trim the edges, and crimp with a fork. Brush the pastry with the beaten egg. Bake for 35 to 40 minutes, or until the pastry is golden.

Makes 8 servings.

Angel Food Cake

At Riversong, we often serve angel food cake with French champagne and Alaska wild berries.

12 extra-large egg whites
  (about 1½ cups)
1¼ teaspoon cream of tartar
¼ teaspoon salt
1½ cups sugar
1¼ cups sifted cake flour
1½ teaspoons vanilla
  extract
Juice of half a lemon
4 cups fresh berries
  (optional)
1 cup heavy cream,
  whipped

Preheat the oven to 350 degrees Fahrenheit. Place the egg whites, cream of tartar, and salt in a large mixing bowl. Beat the egg whites to soft peaks with an electric mixer. Sprinkle 2 tablespoons of the sugar over the surface; gently fold into whipped egg whites. Continue folding in the sugar, 2 tablespoons at a time, until all is incorporated.

Sift 2 tablespoons flour over the surface; gently fold into egg white–sugar mixture. Continue folding in flour 2 tablespoons at a time, until all is incorporated.

Sprinkle the vanilla and lemon juice over the surface; gently fold into the batter. Pour the batter into a 3-quart ungreased angel food cake pan with a removable bottom. Smooth the surface of the batter with a rubber spatula. Rap the pan against a work surface once or twice to remove any air bubbles. Bake for 40 to 45 minutes on the center rack of the oven until the top is golden brown and the cake springs back when pressed.

Remove the cake from the oven and invert it onto a wire rack. Let the cake cool in the pan for 1 hour. Run a knife around the edge of the cake to loosen it. Remove the cake from the pan. Serve with berries, if desired, and whipped cream.

Makes 10 to 12 servings.

Chocolate Bread Pudding

This pudding is probably my favorite dessert. Vanilla ice cream is a perfect accompaniment.

¼ cup unsalted butter

1 pound day-old sourdough bread, cut into 1-inch cubes (about 8 cups)

2 cups heavy cream

1 cup milk

6 ounces bittersweet chocolate, chopped

8 egg yolks

⅔ cup firmly packed light brown sugar

1 teaspoon vanilla extract

1 teaspoon cinnamon

Pinch of salt

Melt the butter in a large, heavy skillet over medium heat. Add the bread cubes and stir until golden brown, about 3 minutes. Transfer the bread cubes to a large bowl; cool slightly. Combine the cream and milk in a heavy, medium saucepan. Bring just to a boil. Remove from heat and add the chocolate. Stir until melted.

Whisk the egg yolks, brown sugar, vanilla, cinnamon, and salt together in another large bowl. Gradually whisk in the warm chocolate mixture. Pour the mixture over the bread. Top with a small plate to keep the bread submerged in the custard. Let the mixture stand until the bread has absorbed almost all the custard, about 1 hour.

Preheat the oven to 325 degrees Fahrenheit. Grease a 9-by-9-by-2-inch baking pan. Pour the bread mixture into the baking pan. Cover the baking pan with foil. Make several small holes in the foil to allow steam to escape. Set the baking pan in a large roasting pan. Add enough hot water to the roasting pan to come 1 inch up the sides of the baking pan. Bake until the custard is set, about 45 minutes. Cool at least 30 minutes on a rack. Serve warm.

Makes 8 servings.

Chocolate Pecan Squares

Like brownies, cookies, and other sweet finger foods, these disappear quickly from the back buffet, where we keep the coffeepots.

2 cups finely chopped pecans
½ cup all-purpose flour
½ teaspoon salt
2 eggs
3 ounces bittersweet
    chocolate
3 tablespoons unsalted
    butter
½ cup sugar
½ cup dark corn syrup
Powdered sugar, for dusting

Preheat the oven to 325 degrees Fahrenheit. Butter an 8-by-8-by-2-inch baking pan.

In a small bowl, mix the pecans with the flour and salt. In a separate small bowl, beat the eggs. Chop the chocolate into small pieces. Put the chocolate and the butter into a large metal bowl and melt over a saucepan of hot water or melt in the top of a double boiler. Set aside to cool.

In a small saucepan, bring the sugar and corn syrup to a boil. Remove the pan from the heat and stir into the cooled chocolate mixture, then stir in the beaten eggs and the pecan mixture.

Pour the batter into the prepared pan and bake on the center rack of the oven for 35 minutes, or until the center of the pan is set. Cool for about 10 minutes, and then cut into 2-inch squares and remove to a wire rack for final cooling. Dust with powdered sugar.

Makes 16 squares.

Summer

Into the Garden

I heard a strange sound one night that I didn't recognize. It was a hollow, slapping sound on the water that seemed to reverberate clear across the river. What I saw from my bedroom window made sense of the sound and made me rush outside in my nightgown. A big, plump beaver had made his way up the riverbank and into the garden. There he sat, perfectly content, eating all the broccoli in sight.

I've had to wage war with more than one creature in my garden. From marauding rabbits to irreverent bears, I've defended my patch of earth with the imperious idea that all that is grown within is solely for human consumption. The geese that we raise and the other animals and birds that find their way to my front yard don't see it that way. Usually, though, enough of everything makes the journey from seed to table (now that I plant an extra row of broccoli).

There is a saying, "When the world wearies, there is always the garden." That is certainly true for the Riversong garden. Things happen, people come and go, but the garden is there, next to the river that will keep on running long after the troubles of the moment are gone. It's a timeless joy. Working in the soil to nurture life from a small seedling must be one of life's most rewarding tasks.

Everyone seems to take delight in munching crisp snow peas from the vine and fat black currants from the bushes near the gate. We pull potatoes in all sizes and colors from the rich earth, spreading them across a burlap blanket to dry in the sun for a day or two. Bushel baskets

overflow with broccoli, carrots, cabbage, and more during harvest. There isn't too much we can't grow from the seedlings I start in flats in the greenhouse, and there isn't anything we won't try.

The only time I ever cried in the garden was the day after the Chernobyl nuclear accident. A warm rain arrived and I rushed out to pull the row covers off the strawberries. I suddenly wondered whether there was any radiation in the rain and stopped in my tracks, not sure whether to cover everything up or to run back in the house. It was a terrible feeling, that an ill wind could bring the problems of people so far away to my garden. I learned later that the radiation from Chernobyl never reached Alaska. But it did affect many other parts of the world— places like Switzerland and Scandinavia, where families like ours took loving care of their broccoli and beans and ran into their gardens when it rained, helpless to protect their plants.

I hope my garden will always be there. And I hope that no ill winds ever blow on the Riversong garden.

Cranberry Ricotta Pancakes

Summer mornings at the lodge are beautiful. The air is crisp, the ground is fresh with the morning dew, and there are flowers everywhere. That's when I especially enjoy serving these pancakes.

2 tablespoons concentrated
   cranberry juice
¾ cup whole milk
6 tablespoons unsalted
   butter
4 eggs
⅔ cup ricotta cheese
1 cup all-purpose flour
2 teaspoons baking powder
½ teaspoon baking soda
¼ teaspoon salt
¼ cup sugar
½ cup chopped cranberries
Unsalted butter and
   maple syrup, as
   accompaniments

In a small nonaluminum saucepan, heat the cranberry juice, milk, and butter until the butter is melted. Transfer to a large mixing bowl. Add the eggs one at a time, beating well after each addition. Fold in the ricotta and cool to room temperature.

Combine the flour, baking powder, baking soda, salt, and sugar in a large bowl. Fold in the egg batter until just mixed. Toss the cranberries in a small amount of additional flour and add to the batter. Cover the batter and let it rest 15 minutes.

Heat the surface of a griddle or skillet. Brush with butter or oil. Pour 3 tablespoons of batter per pancake onto the griddle surface. Cook until the edges of the pancake are dry and the surface is covered with small bubbles. Turn the pancake and cook on the remaining side. Serve the pancakes hot with butter and syrup.

Makes 8 to 12 pancakes.

Vegetable Patties

These patties are great served alongside an entrée salad. You can make them smaller and serve two per person as a first course. Because they are pureed, then sautéed, they are soft and crisp at the same time.

1 pound broccoli, chopped
½ pound green beans, chopped
1 onion, peeled and finely chopped
2 cloves garlic, peeled and minced
2 cups dry sourdough bread crumbs
¼ cup all-purpose flour
2 tablespoons heavy cream
Salt and freshly ground pepper to taste
Canola oil for frying
Chunky mild tomato salsa, as an accompaniment

Cook the broccoli and green beans in a large saucepan of boiling salted water until tender, about 7 minutes. Drain well. Puree the vegetables in a food processor with the onion and garlic. Transfer to a large bowl. Mix in the bread crumbs and flour. Stir in the cream. Season with salt and pepper to taste. Refrigerate the mixture until well chilled, about 1 hour.

Form the mixture into 3-inch balls. Flatten into oval patties.

Heat ¾ inch of oil in a large, heavy skillet over high heat. Add the patties and cook until brown, about 3 minutes per side. Drain on paper towels. Serve the patties with salsa.

Makes 8 large patties, or 8 servings.

Corn for the Grill

The trick to grilling corn is to soak the husks so that they don't burn. The wet husks also release steam, helping to cook the corn.

6 ears sweet corn in husks
6 tablespoons unsalted
  butter, at room
  temperature
6 sprigs fresh herbs, such as
  rosemary or thyme

Soak the corn in a pot of salted water for 1 hour. Start the charcoal in the grill.

Peel the corn husks back without detaching them at the bottom. Remove the silks. Spread the butter on the corn. Remove the leaves from the herb sprigs and coarsely chop, discarding the stems. Sprinkle the herbs over the buttered corn. Pull the husks back around the corn. If the husks are exceptionally limp, tie them in place; otherwise they should hold. Make sure the husks cover the corn completely.

Grill the corn over medium-hot coals, about 6 inches from the heat, rotating periodically, for 10 to 15 minutes.

Makes 6 servings.

Summer Squash with Lamb and Herb Stuffing

This first-course dish offers a Mediterranean slant on Alaskan vegetables. Alaskans enjoy Matanuska Valley–grown lamb, zucchini, onions, and greenhouse-grown tomatoes and bell peppers.

3 tablespoons unsalted butter

2 large zucchini

2 tablespoons olive oil

1 large onion, peeled and finely chopped

1 large green bell pepper, cored, seeded, and finely chopped

1 pound ground lamb

2 large tomatoes, peeled, seeded, and finely chopped

2 small carrots, peeled and finely diced

¼ cup finely chopped fresh purple basil

Salt and freshly ground pepper to taste

1 cup sourdough bread crumbs

2 egg yolks

¼ cup heavy cream

1 cup coarsely shredded Parmesan cheese

Preheat the oven to 350 degrees Fahrenheit. Grease an oblong oven-proof casserole with 2 tablespoons of the unsalted butter. Cut the zucchini in half lengthwise. With a spoon, remove the seeds and enough of the flesh to make a cavity to hold the stuffing.

Heat the olive oil in a medium saucepan. Add the onion and green pepper. Sauté until the onion is translucent and golden. Add the ground lamb and tomatoes and sauté for 6 to 8 minutes, turning the meat occasionally, until it is browned and the moisture from the tomatoes is absorbed.

Remove the pan from the heat. Add the diced carrots and basil. Season with salt and pepper to taste. Set the mixture aside.

Combine the bread crumbs with the egg yolks and cream. Stir the mixture into the lamb sauté, mixing well. Fill the cavities of the squash with the stuffing, mounding slightly. Sprinkle with Parmesan cheese. Dot the top of the zucchini with the remaining 1 tablespoon butter. Place the filled zucchini into the casserole, cover, and bake in the center of the oven for 1 hour, or until the zucchini is tender. Serve immediately.

Makes 4 servings.

Summer Salad with Herb Garden Vinaigrette

Freshly picked greens, salmon cracklings, and a creamy vinaigrette make this salad a summertime delight. Serve it with a chilled, dry white wine.

HERB GARDEN VINAIGRETTE:

2 teaspoons Dijon mustard

Salt and freshly ground
    pepper to taste

¼ cup vinegar

1 cup heavy cream

¼ cup olive oil

2 tablespoons chopped fresh
    chervil

2 tablespoons chopped
    bronze fennel or other
    fennel

SALAD:

Skin of 1 salmon fillet

¼ teaspoon salt

1 head oak-leaf lettuce or
    other leaf lettuce

1½ cups young sorrel leaves

1½ cups young spinach
    leaves

6 mint leaves

1 small red onion, peeled
    and sliced into thin rings

¼ cup garlic chives, chopped

1 tablespoon sunflower seeds

To make the dressing, combine the mustard, salt, pepper, and vinegar. Whisk in the cream and olive oil. Stir in the herbs. This vinaigrette will keep 1 week in the refrigerator. Makes 1½ cups.

To make the salad, preheat the oven to 400 degrees Fahrenheit. Sprinkle the salmon skin with salt. Lay the skin fat side down on a baking sheet and bake for 20 minutes, or until the skin is crisp. Remove the skin from the oven and dice finely. Set aside.

Clean, dry, and shred the lettuce, sorrel, spinach, and mint into a large bowl. Add the red onion, chives, and sunflower seeds. Toss in just enough of the Herb Garden Vinaigrette to lightly coat the lettuce leaves. Garnish with the salmon cracklings. Serve immediately.

Makes 4 to 6 servings.

Wildflower Pasta

I like to serve this pasta with just a little dressing of cream flecked with smoked fish, such as halibut or grayling.

4 cups all-purpose flour
3 large egg yolks
2 large eggs
1 tablespoon olive oil
Pinch of salt
6 tablespoons ice water
1½ cups edible wildflowers,
  such as calendula,
  marigolds, and
  nasturtiums
¼ cup fresh green herbs,
  such as lemon verbena,
  thyme, and mint

Sift the flour into a bowl and make a well in the center. Place the egg yolks, whole eggs, oil, and salt in the well and, using a fork, lightly blend the ingredients until evenly moistened. Add the ice water, a little at a time, to form a smooth dough. Turn the dough out onto a lightly floured surface. Gather into a ball.

Roll the dough out with a pasta machine, or roll by hand with a heavy roller on a lightly floured surface. Roll the pasta into 4 sheets, each 3 inches wide (or as wide as your pasta machine rolls) by 10 inches long, and as thin as you can

roll it without tearing. If the pasta is too wet to roll, sprinkle it with flour and proceed. Cover the sheets of pasta with a dusting of flour, fold gently, and wrap tightly in plastic wrap until ready to use.

Use an assortment of edible flower petals and herbs to mix into the pasta. I think the yellow-orange and pink colors look the best with egg pasta. Purple flowers tend to look a little gray after the pasta has been cooked. Scatter the flowers and herbs evenly onto 2 sheets of the pasta. Wet the edges of the pasta and lay a second sheet of pasta on top of each. Roll the pasta again, as thin as possible, or use a pasta machine at the thinnest setting. Use a sharp knife to cut the pasta into strips, as thin or thick as you desire, depending on the sauce to be used. Drop the pasta gently into lightly salted boiling water and cook for 5 to 7 minutes, or until the pasta is al dente.

Makes 2 pounds, 8 servings.

Edible Flowers in the Riversong Garden

Calendulas—I grow calendulas to dry their yellow-to-orange colored petals for making wildflower pastas and garnishes for soups. The petals taste like lemons.

Marigolds—I grow two types of marigolds, Lemon Gem and Tangerine Gem, that are very aromatic, just like their names. I use their flowers in salads, soups, and iced lemon drinks.

Anise hyssop—Anise hyssop flowers are two-inch lavender spikes that have an aromatic flavor a little bit like licorice. I like to put anise hyssop in clear crab apple jellies because it turns the jelly a beautiful salmon-pink color.

Bee balm—I grow bee balm right next to the anise hyssop. The two flowers in contrast are striking. Bee balm flowers look nearly tropical. They are large pink flowers nearly two inches in diameter, with petals that taste minty. I use them in salads.

Borage—Borage flowers are deep blue stars that look stunning in salads. Remove the sepals from the flower before serving. I also like them sprinkled on dessert plates.

Daylilies—I planted daylily bulbs for their color, but when I discovered their potential as edible flowers and buds, I wouldn't let anyone pick them for the flower arrangements. The petals have an unusual floral taste. We shred them and float them on soups.

Carrots and Onions with Honey and Juniper Berries

The juniper berries add a slight pine flavor to this dish. Dried juniper berries are readily available in stores, but use fresh berries if you can find them. They are much sweeter than the dried ones. This dish is perfect served alongside pork, beef, or game.

10 medium carrots, peeled and thinly sliced
¼ cup red wine vinegar
1 tablespoon honey
1 onion, peeled and thinly sliced
6 to 10 juniper berries, crushed
Salt and freshly ground pepper to taste

Place the carrots in a medium saucepan and cover them with cold water. Add the vinegar, honey, onion, and juniper berries. Season with salt and pepper to taste. Simmer the mixture over medium heat until the carrots are just tender and the liquid is reduced. Drain the liquid from the carrots and onions and serve.

Makes 4 to 6 servings.

Danish Cabbage Rolls

My grandmother used to make these cabbage rolls with white rice and beef. I've changed her recipe a little by using cranberries, brown rice, and veal.

1 large green cabbage
1 large onion, peeled and
   minced
1 large egg
1½ pounds ground veal
½ cup coarsely chopped
   cranberries
½ cup cooked brown rice
1½ cups homemade or
   canned chicken stock
1 cup minced mushrooms
1 tablespoon flour
½ cup sour cream
Salt and freshly ground
   pepper to taste

Clean the cabbage, removing any discolored outer leaves. Select 12 of the largest leaves from the cabbage. Bring 4 quarts of salted water to a rapid boil. Drop the cabbage leaves gently into the water. Blanch for 2 minutes. Remove the leaves carefully and drain on paper towels.

In a bowl, combine the onion, egg, veal, and cranberries, mixing well. Add the rice. Place about ¼ cup of the veal mixture onto the lower half of one cabbage leaf, in the center. Fold both sides of the leaf over the veal mixture. Fold up the bottom of the leaf and roll up tightly. Repeat the process with the remaining veal and cabbage leaves.

Place the cabbage rolls seam side down in a wide saucepan large enough to hold the 12 rolls. Pour the chicken stock over the rolls. Bring to a boil over medium heat. Reduce heat, cover, and simmer for 1 hour. Add additional stock, if necessary. Remove the rolls and keep warm, leaving the remaining stock in the saucepan.

Add the mushrooms to the saucepan and bring to a simmer. Add the flour and cook until mushrooms are tender, about 2 minutes. Add the sour cream and season with salt and pepper. Serve the sauce warm over cabbage rolls.

Makes 6 to 8 servings.

Rose Petal Almond Cupcakes

Wild rose petals taste a little like almonds when they are baked. I love them in baked goods, fresh salads, and even iced tea.

CUPCAKES:
1 cup all-purpose flour
½ cup ground almonds
1¼ teaspoons baking powder
Pinch of salt
⅓ cup vegetable shortening
½ cup granulated sugar
1 large egg
⅓ cup water
½ cup fresh rose petals

FROSTING:
1 cup powdered sugar
1½ tablespoons unsalted butter
½ teaspoon almond extract

To make the cupcakes, preheat the oven to 350 degrees Fahrenheit. Line 12 muffin tins with paper cups. In a small bowl, stir together the flour, almonds, baking powder, and salt. In a large bowl, cream together the shortening and granulated sugar. Beat in the egg. Add the flour mixture alternately with the water. Gently fold in the rose petals, reserving a few petals for decoration.

Divide the batter among the 12 muffin tins, filling the cups two-thirds full. Bake on the center rack of the oven for 15 to 20 minutes, or until a skewer inserted in the center comes out clean. Allow the cupcakes to cool.

To make the frosting, beat together the powdered sugar, butter, and almond extract until the mixture is fluffy. Spread on the cupcakes, pressing a few rose petals onto the top.

Makes 12 cupcakes.

Honey Marinade for Fish

I'm a big fan of using honey whenever possible. This marinade keeps the fish moist and tender, as well as adding the sweetness of honey to tart and spicy flavors.

½ cup rice vinegar
½ cup fresh lime juice
¼ cup canola oil
1 tablespoon Alaska
   fireweed, or other, honey
1 tablespoon Oriental chili
   oil
1 teaspoon sesame seed

Combine all ingredients and mix well. I store marinades and dressings in bottles that have ceramic and wire caps, so that they can be mixed and stored easily.

Use to marinate salmon or halibut for at least 1 hour, or rockfish overnight.

Makes 1¼ cups.

The Long Journey

The Japanese couple weren't sure what kind of day they were going to have at the lodge. Prompted by a brochure or an ad, or perhaps by a comment from a friend back in Tokyo, they found themselves transported from the bustle of city life in Japan to the Yentna River. A guide was there with a boat to meet their floatplane, and was holding on to the ropes that kept the aircraft and boat from drifting apart in the moving current. The two held on to each other as they steadied themselves in the boat. This quiet couple had traveled thousands of miles to try their luck at fishing for the mighty Alaska king salmon.

King, or chinook, salmon is the largest species of salmon that runs up Lake Creek. During their lives, the fish travel an incredible distance from river to ocean and then back again to the waters where they were spawned. Kings in our river can be as large as 60 pounds. It's an amazing story from beginning to end. As soon as the winter ice washes away to the sea, the fish begin to return to the river. Kings are the most sought after of all the salmon species.

Like the seabirds overhead, people seem to follow the fish on their inland journey from the sea back to the river. Somehow, people from nearly every corner of the earth find their way to our front door, eager to experience the phenomenon of Alaska sportfishing.

Not every person who visits our lodge is a good fisherman. For some, like the couple from Tokyo, fishing might be a once-in-a-lifetime experience. But this particular couple would have a more memorable

experience than most. Once they were anchored securely in their designated fishing spot the next day, guide and guests began readying themselves, baiting hooks and checking gear.

Before they could even set their lines in the water, a giant king salmon jumped into the boat, creating confusion and havoc. A fish thrashing in a small 18-foot boat can be a hazard, even causing the boat to tip over, so the guide promptly bonked the huge salmon on the head with his wooden paddle. The startled couple were elated. Even though the fish was not taken by any usual angling technique, it was still their fish.

That salmon must have traveled thousands of miles over the course of its five-year life span, surviving many a sea adventure against marauding sea mammals or the fisher's net. What are the odds of a fish returning to its spawning grounds only to make a spectacular leap into the air and land in a fishing boat? What was a lucky story for the anglers was not such a lucky story for the fish.

A week later, the Japanese couple were enjoying their salmon at a party back in Tokyo.

Thai-style Tapioca Soup

I lived in Southeast Asia as a young girl, and I've always had a taste for Asian foods. We normally think of tapioca as a dessert, but it is a great thickener and unusual addition for soups.

7 cups homemade or canned chicken stock
½ pound ground pork
1 teaspoon salt
1 teaspoon freshly ground pepper
¼ cup large pearl tapioca
⅔ pound flaked, cooked crabmeat
1 small Chinese (Nappa) cabbage, finely shredded
1 tablespoon soy sauce, or to taste

In a large saucepan, bring the chicken stock to a boil over medium heat. Add the pork, salt, and pepper, stirring well to break up the pork. Reduce the heat and add the tapioca. Simmer for 15 to 20 minutes, or until the pork is cooked. Add the crabmeat and cabbage to the soup. Continue to simmer for 1 to 2 minutes, or until the crabmeat is heated through. Remove from the heat and stir in the soy sauce. Serve immediately.

Makes 6 to 8 servings.

Green Bean Salad with Soy-Sesame Dressing

This dressing can be used on any cooked vegetable or fresh salad. It also makes a good marinade for fish.

SOY-SESAME DRESSING:
1½ cups canola oil
6 large cloves garlic, peeled and minced
2 tablespoons minced fresh ginger
½ cup fresh lemon juice
½ cup soy sauce
¼ cup sesame oil

SALAD:
4 cups green beans
1 teaspoon salt
1 tablespoon sesame seeds
Half a lemon

To make the dressing, heat the canola oil in a small saucepan. Add the garlic and sauté until it is light brown in color. Cool the garlic–oil mixture, then whisk in the ginger, lemon juice, soy sauce, and sesame oil. The dressing can be stored in the refrigerator for up to a month. Makes 2½ cups.

Bring about 4 quarts of water to a rolling boil in a large saucepan over high heat. Add the salt. Clip the tough ends of the green beans and remove any fibrous strings. Add the beans to the water in small amounts so that the water returns quickly to a boil. Blanch the beans for 3 to 5 minutes, depending on the size of the beans, until they are crisp-tender. Remove the beans and place them in a large bowl of ice water to stop them from cooking. Remove the beans from the water and pat dry.

When ready to serve, toss lightly in just enough of the Soy-Sesame Dressing to coat the beans. Sprinkle the sesame seeds over the beans. Cut the lemon into slices, then into wedges, and toss into the beans. Serve the beans warm or chilled.

Makes 4 to 6 servings.

Noodles with Daylily Buds

Daylilies are hardy in the Riversong area of Alaska. Last year, I discovered what the Chinese have known for centuries—that the buds are as delicious as the flowers. My geese compete with me for the buds in early summer.

1 cup daylily buds
3 tablespoons unsalted
   butter
½ cup coarsely chopped
   green onions
1 teaspoon chopped fresh
   thyme
Salt and freshly ground
   pepper to taste
1 pound Smoked Salmon
   Noodles (see page 161),
   or fettuccine
¼ cup shredded Parmesan
   cheese

Bring 4 quarts of salted water to a rapid boil. Rinse the daylily buds and pat dry. In a large sauté pan, heat the butter over medium heat. Add the daylily buds. Sauté for 2 to 3 minutes. Add the green onions and thyme. Season with salt and pepper to taste.

Add the noodles to the boiling water. Cook until the noodles are al dente, 3 to 5 minutes. Drain the noodles and add to the daylily buds. Sprinkle with the Parmesan cheese. Serve hot.

Makes 4 to 6 servings.

Japanese Eggplant Ratatouille

When I was in France, I had a lovely meal in which the ratatouille was served arranged like a flower, with chives for the stem and two beautiful fillets of fish for the leaves. I was on my way to Japan, so I kept the image with me and replicated it for a dinner I cooked there. Use ratatouille as a side dish, serving it in a small mound on the plate.

1 large red onion, peeled and diced
½ cup olive oil
1 red pepper, diced
1 large green pepper, diced
4 small Japanese eggplants, diced
3 small zucchini, diced
3 tomatoes, peeled, seeded, and coarsely chopped
¼ cup minced fresh basil or perilla
1 clove garlic, peeled and minced
Salt and freshly ground pepper to taste

In a large skillet over medium heat, sauté the onion in the olive oil until soft and translucent. Add the red and green peppers and eggplants and cook 5 minutes, stirring often. Add the zucchini and tomatoes and simmer for 15 minutes. Add the basil and garlic and simmer an additional 10 minutes. Season with salt and pepper to taste. Serve warm.

Makes 4 to 6 servings.

How to Clean a Fish

Get a Grip—When landing a fish, it's best to use a net. Whether you plan to release or eat it, never lift a fish by its tail, which tends to pull the flesh away from the spine and can cause pockets of blood to pool. Instead, handle the fish by its head, and try not to puncture the flesh, which can introduce bacteria.

Stun Your Fish—The quality of a fish deteriorates the moment it leaves the water. Immediately stun the fish with a small fish club or rock to prevent it from flopping, which can bruise its flesh. Bruising will cause blood to leak into the flesh, decreasing edibility. Bruising also causes rapid rancidity. Never leave your catch in the sun, trail it behind your raft on a stringer, or dry it out on the floor of your boat. Burlap sacks will best protect fish until mealtime.

Bleed Your Fish—It is critical to bleed fish as soon as possible, even if you can't clean your catch right away, because fish blood contaminates the flesh. Lift the gill cover and stick your knife behind the gills in the throat area. This severs the blood vessels and arteries around the head. Allow the fish to bleed for 20 minutes, wash it, then cover and chill if possible.

Five Steps to Cleaning a Fish

1. Insert the tip of your knife into the vent opening behind the anal fin, and make a shallow cut along the belly to the point where the pectoral fins join the body—without touching internal organs.
2. Cut the connective tissue at the vent and throat and the insides should fall out. Use your index finger as a guide if necessary.

3. Remove the gills by slitting the connective tissue between the gills on the bottom side of the fish. Run your knife around the gills and to the bottom on both sides of the fish. Twist out the gills with your hands.

4. Remove the kidney. (It looks like a thin clot of blood along the spine.) Run your knife down both edges of the kidney and scoop it out. A small spoon works well for this.

5. Rinse the fish well in clean water and pat dry. Some fish, such as grayling and perch, should be scaled before cooking. Take the edge of your knife, hold your fish by the tail, and scrape toward the head, the direction opposite from the way the scales lie.

Smoked Salmon Noodles

I used this recipe as one of my entries for a food contest sponsored by the Hankyu Corporation of Osaka, Japan. I won first place and a trip to Japan! Dress these noodles with butter and soy sauce, and serve with lemon wedges.

1½ cups all-purpose flour
2 eggs
Pinch of salt
½ cup finely chopped
  kippered salmon

Place the flour on a clean work surface and make a well in it. Add the eggs and salt. With a fork, beat the eggs into the flour. Before all the egg is completely mixed in, add the salmon and continue to mix.

Gather the dough into a ball, adding a teaspoon of water at a time, if necessary, to make a cohesive dough. Knead the dough until it becomes smooth and elastic, about 10 minutes. Cover the dough with plastic wrap and let it rest for 15 minutes. If rolling the dough by hand, place the dough on a floured surface. Use a rolling pin to roll the dough out to ¼-inch thickness. Cut the noodles into ¼-inch strips. If using a pasta machine, roll the dough according to the manufacturer's directions.

Bring a large pot of salted water to a rapid boil over medium-high heat. Add the noodles. Reduce the heat to a simmer and keep the noodles in the water for 5 to 7 minutes, or until they are al dente. Drain the noodles and serve.

Makes 4 servings.

Halibut with Sake Kasu

Kasu is the "lees," or dregs, of the rice left when sake is made. It can be purchased in Japanese specialty food shops. Pieces of kasu look like bread dough when purchased. Kasu recipes are handed down through families and jealously guarded. The kasu and sugar in this recipe caramelize the fish. This marinade can be used with salmon and cod as well.

1 cup sake kasu
½ cup sugar
1½ cups sweet rice wine
2 pounds fresh halibut
    fillets

Pulse the sake kasu and sugar in a food processor until well blended. Add the wine and process to a paste. Spread half of the mixture over the bottom of a 9-by-13-inch baking dish. Place the halibut in a single layer in the dish; rub the remaining mixture over the fish. Cover and refrigerate the fish overnight.

Heat a griddle or large nonstick skillet. Remove the halibut from the marinade, rinse lightly, and pat dry. Sear the fish, cooking for approximately 4 minutes on each side, turning once. Serve immediately.

Makes 4 servings.

Steamed Salmon in Paper

This recipe is another I submitted to the Hankyu Corporation recipe contest. Cooking in sealed paper packets steams the fish so that it remains moist.

4 skinless, boned salmon fillets (6 ounces each)
1 large carrot, julienned
1 leek, julienned
2 tablespoons mirin (Japanese rice wine)
2 teaspoons sesame oil
2 tablespoons soy sauce
2 tablespoons sesame seeds
2 tablespoons lemon juice

Oil 4 sheets of parchment paper, each large enough to enclose one fillet. Place a salmon fillet in the center of each sheet. Divide the carrot and leek among the 4 fillets, layering them on top of the fish. Sprinkle each fillet equally with the mirin, sesame oil, soy sauce, sesame seeds, and lemon juice.

Fold the bottom of the parchment paper up over the fillet. Bring in the sides, tucking in the excess folds. Fold the top of the paper down and under the edge like an envelope, sealing well so that the juices won't leak out.

Steam the packets for 8 to 10 minutes. Open the packets and arrange the fish on individual plates before serving.

Makes 4 servings.

Asian Fish Stock

Who says all stocks and sauces have to be classic French? This stock is wonderful to have on hand. Simmer it with your favorite Asian ingredients to make a soup. Try adding halibut or other chunks of firm fish, carrots, green onion, Asian noodles, and fresh cilantro (coriander) for a delicious lunchtime meal.

1 pound halibut trimmings
   (head and bones)
2 onions, peeled and
   coarsely chopped
2 stalks celery, coarsely
   chopped
1 leek, chopped
2 tablespoons white
   peppercorns
¼ cup chopped fresh cilantro
   (coriander)
4 lime leaves
1-inch piece fresh ginger
Salt and freshly ground
   white pepper to taste
8 cups water

Combine all ingredients in a large stockpot. Bring to a boil, then reduce the heat and simmer, covered, for 1 hour. Skim the fat from the surface from time to time. Strain through a fine-mesh sieve. Discard the bones and other residue. Strain the stock again through layers of cheesecloth.

Cool the stock, then refrigerate. Remove any additional fat from the surface before using. This stock can be frozen for up to 3 months.

Makes 1½ quarts.

Homemade Korean Kim Chee

We're always delighted when we can surprise our guests by serving them something special. Korean guests over the years have given us high praise for serving this meal accompaniment popular in their country. Kim chee is a spicy cabbage condiment that goes well with rice and fish dishes.

1 medium Chinese (Nappa)
   cabbage
½ cup coarse or kosher salt
2 green onions, chopped
3 tablespoons chopped hot
   red peppers
1 tablespoon sugar
1 teaspoon chopped fresh
   ginger

Shred the cabbage coarsely into a large bowl. Add the salt and about 4 cups of water to cover. Soak the cabbage in the brine for 4 hours. Drain well.

Combine the green onions, hot peppers, sugar, and ginger. The flavor of kim chee develops a little more if it is allowed to rest in the refrigerator for 24 hours before serving. For longer storage, it is best to preserve the cabbage in hot, sterilized jars because the odor can be strong. Serve cold or cool from the refrigerator. It will keep for 1 month in the refrigerator.

Makes 6 to 8 cups.

Thick and Sweet Soy Sauce

When I was a teenager, I had a friend whose grandmother made homemade soy sauce. It was sweet, thick, and rich. We would make a meal out of hot bowls of white rice topped with butter and the soy sauce.

2 tablespoons honey
1½ cups all-purpose soy
   sauce
½ cup dark molasses
2 tablespoons lemon juice
1 tablespoon grated fresh
   ginger

Combine all the ingredients in a medium saucepan over medium heat. Bring to a boil, then reduce the heat to low. Continue cooking until the soy sauce mixture is reduced by half. Remove from heat and cool. Strain the liquid and pour the soy sauce into a clean bottle or jar. Secure the top with a cap or lid. This sauce will keep for 1 month in the refrigerator.

Makes 1 cup.

Yvette's Party

It was dinner time. The three café tables in the greenhouse were covered with bright cotton linens, graced with wildflowers, and ready for guests. The lodge was bustling with activity as fishermen, flushed with excitement and pleasure, returned to camp carrying their catch of prized Alaska salmon. Georges and Yvette Bouteiller were already seated at a table. A bottle of fine California cabernet had been poured, just as Georges had requested for each meal.

Georges and Yvette live in Paris, near Montmartre and the Sacré-Coeur on a small, picturesque street called rue de Turgot. A heavy wooden door keeps passersby from seeing their elegant foyer and atrium.

When Yvette shops for food in Paris, she goes down crowded streets to favorite specialty shops—one for meats, and another that sells only chocolates and jams. The bustle of daily life on rue de Turgot is worlds apart from that at Riversong, but the change from the Parisian lights to the candle glow of Lake Creek must be a pleasing one for the Bouteillers. They come each summer to fish for king and silver salmon, spending their nights in a tiny, rustic cabin.

Christine McEnery, our chef for the season, had delivered the first course to their table. Christine had spent some time in France and was always trying to improve her French with the Bouteillers. When she returned to the kitchen, she whispered that Georges had told her it was Yvette's birthday. That set the party in motion.

We quickly chilled a small bottle of Veuve Clicquot champagne, and Christine made an elegant little cake for Yvette with her name scrolled in chocolate on the rim of the white plate. The entire staff gathered in the greenhouse and sang a rousing round of "Happy Birthday." Yvette looked surprised, and then she cried in joy and hugged each one of us. It was a beautiful birthday celebration.

Several days later, I happened to be looking through the fishing licenses we had issued that week and noticed Yvette's license. My eyes widened as I read that her birthday was not in June. I quickly consulted with Christine in the kitchen, and we laughed until tears streamed from our eyes. What had Georges meant to tell Christine? And what must Yvette have thought when we all came clamoring into the greenhouse to sing "Happy Birthday" to her? It became one of the most charming stories of the season.

One winter we went to visit the Bouteillers in Paris. Our daughters saw the *Mona Lisa*, I took cooking classes at the Cordon Bleu, Carl visited travel agents, and we all got to see the stunning sight of the Sacré-Coeur, lit up against the night.

One evening recently, as we were flying to Anchorage in a small Cessna 206, our daughter Amanda pressed her face against the window, eager for the first sight of the city. As it came into view, she turned to me and said, "Oh, look, Mom. It looks just like Paris at night."

Normandy Carrot Soup

I traveled with Georges and Yvette throughout Normandy, where Yvette lived as a child. We had lunch in a beautiful little village called Honfleur, where we ate at a charming restaurant called Hostellerie le Chat. Cider is an old-fashioned Norman ingredient not used as much in modern French cooking, but well worth remembering.

¼ cup unsalted butter
2 pounds small carrots,
    peeled and cut into
    1-inch pieces
2 medium yellow onions,
    peeled and thinly sliced
1½ cups apple cider
1 tablespoon cider vinegar
6 cups homemade or canned
    chicken stock
Salt and freshly ground
    white pepper to taste
Half an apple, finely
    shredded, for garnish

In a large saucepan, melt the butter over medium heat and add the carrots, onions, cider, and vinegar. Simmer over low heat for 15 minutes, or until the carrots are tender. Add the chicken stock and simmer for 10 minutes.

Remove the soup from the heat and puree in batches in a food processor. Season with salt and pepper to taste. Serve in warm bowls with the apple garnish.

Makes 4 to 6 servings.

Alaska Cold-cured Salmon

Georges and Yvette do not like their salmon cured too strongly. Our Riversong salmon rivals the best. This recipe involves a two-day process.

1 large salmon fillet (2 to
　3 pounds)
2 tablespoons olive oil
¼ cup chopped fresh dill
1 cup sugar
⅔ cup salt
1 tablespoon freshly ground
　black pepper
1 tablespoon dried dill
1 tablespoon chopped fresh
　cilantro (coriander)
1 tablespoon chopped fresh
　parsley
Grated peel of 2 lemons
Grated peel of 2 oranges
1 teaspoon fennel seeds
1 teaspoon fresh thyme
　leaves
Capers, chopped hard-
　cooked egg, sliced red
　onion, and toasted
　French bread as
　accompaniments

Skin the salmon, remove any pin bones, place it on a bread cooling rack, and then transfer rack and fish to a pan to fit. Rub the salmon with 1 tablespoon of the olive oil and 2 tablespoons of the fresh dill. Let stand at room temperature for 15 minutes.

Mix the sugar, salt, pepper, dried dill, cilantro, parsley, lemon and orange peel, fennel seeds, thyme, and remaining 2 tablespoons fresh dill in a bowl. Pour the mixture over the salmon to coat completely. Allow the salmon to stand in the refrigerator, covered with wrap (do not let it touch the salmon), for 24 hours.

Remove the salmon from the mixture, rub with the remaining 1 tablespoon olive oil, put the salmon in a dry pan and let stand, chilled, for 24 hours.

Slice the salmon thin and serve with capers, chopped hard-cooked egg, and sliced red onion with toasted French bread. The cured salmon keeps 4 to 5 days in the refrigerator.

Makes 8 to 10 appetizer servings.

Beets with Black Currants

In the Riversong garden, we grow a type of spring onion called "Santa Claus" that is a vibrant red color. If they're in season, stir them together with the currants, bacon, and herbs. This beet dish is wonderful served with rabbit, salmon, or lamb.

1 cup fresh black (Swedish) or other currants

4 large red beets

3 tablespoons unsalted butter

1 clove garlic, peeled and minced

2 tablespoons cider vinegar

¼-inch slice Canadian bacon, diced and fried crisp

2 tablespoons minced fresh lemon verbena (or other favorite herb)

Salt and freshly ground pepper to taste

Preheat the oven to 400 degrees Fahrenheit. Wash and pick over the currants. Slice the currants in half. Wrap each beet in aluminum foil. Bake the beets until they are tender, about 1 hour. Remove from the oven, peel off the outer skin with a small, sharp knife, and dice into ½-inch pieces.

In a skillet, heat the butter. Add the garlic and sauté for 2 minutes. Add the beets and vinegar, tossing well to coat the beets thoroughly. When the beets are heated through, add the currants, bacon, and herbs. Toss the mixture lightly and season with salt and pepper to taste.

Makes 4 to 6 servings.

Salmon Puffs with Basil and Cheese

This finger food dish is a tasty appetizer or first course. We keep feta on hand all spring and summer in a large bucket of brine down in the root cellar.

½ cup Danish or other feta cheese, crumbled

½ cup plain yogurt

½ cup chopped fresh basil

1 cup cooked, flaked salmon

Salt and freshly ground pepper to taste

14-ounce package frozen puff pastry (preferably made with butter, not vegetable oil), thawed

1 egg, beaten

Preheat the oven to 425 degrees Fahrenheit. Line a baking sheet with parchment paper. Combine the cheese, yogurt, basil, and salmon in a medium bowl. Season to taste with the salt and pepper.

Roll the puff pastry out on a clean, floured surface. Using a 4-inch round cookie cutter (or a clean 3½-inch-diameter tuna can), cut out 16 or more circles from the dough. (Cut an even number of circles.) Place half of the rounds onto the baking sheet. Spoon a tablespoon of the cheese mixture onto the center of each round. Brush the edge of each pastry circle with some of the beaten egg. Top each circle with a second round of pastry. Pinch the edges together to seal. Make a small slit in the top of each round. Glaze the pastries with the remaining beaten egg. Bake for 15 minutes or until well browned and crisp. Serve warm.

Makes 8 puffs.

Grilled Red Snapper with Fennel and Cream

The fennel in this dish gives the fish a haunting anise flavor. Georges and Yvette ordered this in the little restaurant by the water at Honfleur. The restaurant was preparing for a wedding reception that night, and everything was decorated in yellow.

3 tablespoons unsalted
   butter
1 small onion, peeled and
   thinly sliced
1 fennel or anise bulb,
   thinly sliced
¼ cup heavy cream
1 teaspoon vinegar
¼ teaspoon fennel seeds
2 tablespoons olive oil
2 red snapper fillets
   (8 ounces each)
Melted unsalted butter for
   basting the fish
Salt and freshly ground
   pepper to taste

Melt the butter in a medium skillet over medium heat. Add the onion and fennel. Sauté for 10 minutes, or until the fennel is tender, stirring occasionally. Stir in the cream, vinegar, and fennel seeds. Set aside.

Heat the olive oil on a griddle or in a wide skillet. Fry the snapper, starting skin side down, for 3 minutes on each side, basting with a small amount of butter. Season with salt and pepper. Place the fillets on plates and cover with the fennel cream sauce. Serve immediately.

Makes 2 servings.

Favorite Herbs in the Riversong Garden

Bronze fennel—The leaves of this golden, feathery plant have an anise flavor. We use bronze fennel with meats such as lamb and in salads like Hot Danish Potato Salad. It is also good in herb breads and pasta dishes.

Chervil—Chervil has a delicate flavor that goes well with fish and eggs. We like to make a chervil-garlic dressing to serve with tomato and green bean salad.

Lemon verbena—This is my favorite herb. Its citrusy flavor makes it good in soups, salads, cakes, and iced lemon drinks. I grow this tender herb in pots on the front porch, then bring it indoors and nurture it throughout the winter.

Perilla—Perilla is a cousin to basil, and we use it similarly. In Japan, purple perilla is poached with apricots to turn the fruit a beautiful scarlet color. Try spreading a sheet of nori (seaweed) with sesame oil, then sprinkling it with perilla. Toast the nori in the oven, and then cut it into strips and use as a garnish for soups and salads.

Sweet cicely—Besides mint, this is the hardiest herb in our garden. Our sweet cicely has survived uprooting, floods, and 60-below weather. The roots can be cooked and pureed or deep-fried and eaten like potato chips.

Sweet woodruff—This dainty herb grows quickly in the garden and spreads readily. The delicate flowers taste like honey and vanilla; we use them as a garnish.

Smoked Salmon Fromage Blanc

We serve this cheese appetizer spread thinly on crackers or toasted French bread. The combination of cheese and herb flavors can be varied to suit your mood. Smoked grayling or halibut can be tasty substitutions for the salmon. It is best served after a spectacular day of Alaska fishing, along with a cold flute of French champagne.

8 ounces cream cheese
8 ounces cottage cheese
8 ounces ricotta cheese
2 cloves garlic, peeled and
  minced
3 tablespoons minced fresh
  dill
1 tablespoon minced fresh
  chervil
1 tablespoon minced fresh
  garlic chives
½ pound kippered salmon,
  finely minced
1½ cups heavy cream
Salt and freshly ground
  pepper to taste

Strain the cream cheese, cottage cheese, and ricotta cheese through a sieve.

In a large bowl, combine the cheeses, garlic, herbs, and salmon. Whip the heavy cream until it forms soft peaks. Add to the cheese mixture and fold in gently. Add salt and pepper to taste.

Divide the cheese in half. Place the mixture in two small cheesecloth-lined bowls. Tie the cheesecloths over a long, sturdy skewer, centering the cheese bundles on the skewer. Set the skewer across a bowl or pot deep enough so the cheese can drain. Refrigerate overnight to allow the cheese to drain and firm up. Remove the cheesecloth and serve. The cheese will keep for 2 to 3 days in the refrigerator.

Makes 2 cheese balls, 1 pound each.

Reindeer Ragoût

If reindeer meat isn't available, use beef or moose meat in this recipe. Reindeer can be purchased commercially in Alaska.

2 tablespoons canola oil

2 medium onions, peeled and coarsely chopped

3 pounds reindeer chuck, cut into ½-inch cubes

1 clove garlic, peeled and minced

½ teaspoon caraway seeds

2 tablespoons sweet paprika

2½ quarts beer, at room temperature, flat

Salt and freshly ground pepper to taste

1 pound potatoes, scrubbed and diced

1 medium tomato, peeled, seeded, and coarsely chopped

2 green peppers, seeded and coarsely chopped

2 teaspoons hot pepper sauce

Heat the oil in a large, heavy saucepan over medium heat. Add the onions and sauté until translucent. Add the meat and sear until brown on all sides.

Remove the pan from the heat and add the garlic, caraway seeds, and paprika. Add the beer and stir well. Season to taste with salt and pepper.

Return to the heat, cover, and simmer over medium heat for 1 hour. Add the potatoes, tomato, peppers, and hot pepper sauce, adding more beer or water if needed. Simmer the ragoût until the vegetables are tender, about 20 minutes. Serve in warmed bowls.

Makes 6 servings.

Yvette's Twelfth Night Cake

Twelfth Night, celebrated January 6, is a holiday of religious significance in France. When Carl and I were in France, it was close to Twelfth Night, and these lovely cakes were being sold everywhere. We were visiting with our friends the Bouteillers, and Yvette served us one. Carl found the little charm hidden inside and his prize was to wear a golden paper crown on his head for the rest of the evening. This buttery pastry is also called gâteau des rois, or kings' cake.

1 sheet frozen puff pastry, thawed

3 tablespoons unsalted butter, melted

1 whole almond

Preheat the oven to 425 degrees Fahrenheit. Line a baking sheet with parchment paper. Roll the puff pastry out into a circle, about 1 inch thick and 8 inches in diameter. Place the pastry on a baking sheet. Brush the top of the pastry completely with butter. Push the almond down into the pastry. Trace a lattice pattern on the top of the pastry with a sharp knife. Bake on the center rack of the oven for 12 to 15 minutes, or until the pastry is golden brown. Serve in wedges and reward the finder of the almond with a special treat.

Makes 6 to 8 servings.

Note: Use caution. Look for the almond, so you don't choke on it. In France, a small bean or charm is used instead of a whole almond. This cake can be decorated with favorite confections and filled with frangipane or custard if desired.

Pears Baked with Cardamom

Serve these rich, sweet pears on a dessert plate with a couple of small home-made cookies. You can also use them to make a pear tart.

3 large pears, peeled,
halved, and cored
2 tablespoons brown sugar
½ cup orange liqueur
2 teaspoons ground
cardamom

Preheat the oven to 350 degrees Fahrenheit. Cut each pear half into thin slices, leaving the small end attached, and spread the slices like a fan. Arrange them in a shallow, oven-proof dish and sprinkle them with the brown sugar. Pour the liqueur over the pears, and sprinkle with cardamom. Place the dish in the oven and bake for 40 minutes, or until the pears are tender.

Makes 6 servings.

Black Currant Pastries with White Chocolate Sauce

Black currant bushes grow near our garden gate. I love their plump, sweet berries with just a hint of tartness. Sometimes we use this filling to make a black currant–white chocolate tart with a dark chocolate crust. Don't overbake the puff pastry; it should be tender, not brittle.

6 ounces white chocolate,
  chopped
6 large egg yolks
1½ cups sugar
2 sheets frozen puff pastry,
  thawed
1 egg, beaten
½ teaspoon cardamom
½ cup finely chopped black
  walnuts
4 cups coarsely chopped
  black currants
¼ cup unsalted butter
3 tablespoons crème de cassis
  liqueur
1 cup chilled heavy cream
black currants and fresh
  mint leaves for garnish

Melt the white chocolate in the top of a double boiler. Stir constantly until it is smooth. Remove from double boiler top and set aside. Wash the double boiler top.

Beat the egg yolks and 6 tablespoons of the sugar in a mixer until light and fluffy. Place the mixture into the top of the double boiler and bring to a simmer over medium-low heat. Whisk for about 5 minutes until the mixture has thickened. Whisk in the melted white chocolate. Remove from the heat and cool to room temperature, and then refrigerate, covered with plastic wrap, until needed.

Preheat the oven to 375 degrees Fahrenheit. Roll out each sheet of pastry on a lightly floured surface into a 10-by-12-inch rectangle. Cut each rectangle into 8 equal pieces. Transfer the pastries to a large baking sheet. Brush the pastries with the beaten egg. Prick the surface of the pastries with a fork. In a small bowl, mix together the cardamom and ½ cup of the sugar. Sprinkle each pastry with the sugar mixture and walnuts, lightly pressing the nuts into the dough. Bake the pastries on the center rack of the oven for

continued on next page

15 minutes, or until just golden. Remove to a rack and let cool.

When ready to serve, heat the black currants, butter, crème de cassis, and 4 tablespoons of sugar in a sauté pan until the berries have sweetened slightly, about 5 minutes. Whip the cream until it is thick and forms soft peaks. Gently fold the whipped cream into the white chocolate mixture.

Place one pastry on each of 8 plates. Spread each of the 8 pastries with ½ cup of the black currant sauce, then with ½ cup of the whipped cream–white chocolate mixture. Top with a second pastry. Garnish with additional black currants rolled in remaining sugar and mint leaves.

Makes 8 servings.

Carl's Calling

The opening line of Robert Service's poem *The Cremation of Sam McGee* reads: "There are strange things done in the midnight sun / By the men who moil for gold; the Arctic trails have their secret tales / That would make your blood run cold. . . ." In the poem, Service vividly captures the mystique and spirit of the gold rush days in Alaska. Although those days are long gone, strange things are still done under the midnight sun.

The ritual of fishing at Riversong begins every day at the boathouse. Rods and reels are assembled, tennis shoes are exchanged for hip waders, and fishing vests are filled with special, colorful lures. The sight of the boat landing is pleasant in the morning sun. Guides and guests bustle about, preparing for the day.

One morning, after everything was assembled, Carl set off from the boathouse with a couple from New York and headed for a favorite fishing spot downriver from the lodge. It was a crisp, late summer morning, and the tall cottonwoods lining the bank were gently swaying in the breeze. It was silver salmon season, a time in summer when a hint of yellow tints the leaves and animals begin to make early preparations for the winter.

As the fishing party traveled east from the lodge, a huge flock of Arctic terns swooped down upon the boat, threatening Carl and his guests. The boat had passed too close to their nesting area for the terns' liking.

These small white birds make an incredible migratory journey every year. They fly from Alaska to Antarctica and back again, a trip more than 30,000 miles long. It's an amazing sight to see the small birds defiantly attack eagles three times their size, not to mention boatloads of people.

Carl finally arrived at the fishing spot, having entertained his guests on the way with a long tale about how one could attract male moose by making a particular noise. Well, this is true, but Carl had never actually done it before. Undaunted by his lack of experience, he proceeded to demonstrate his most eloquent moose call. To the amazement of his guests, and most of all himself, a huge male moose came crashing through the woods looking for what he took to be a female. Carl's guests must have thought him an expert moose caller.

Yes, there are strange things done here in the land of the midnight sun: Arctic terns protect their nests from eagles and men, and male moose look for their females, but find a surprised male human instead.

Hot Danish Potato Salad

Every Sunday in the summer, we have a barbecue at the lodge with lots of fresh salmon, grilled corn, and, of course, potato salad.

2 pounds potatoes
½ pound Danish ham, cooked and diced
1 tablespoon chopped fresh dill
1 cup sour cream
½ cup cottage cheese
½ cup Danish blue cheese
Salt and freshly ground pepper to taste
4 green onions, chopped

Thoroughly scrub and trim any blemishes from the potatoes. Cut the potatoes into quarters and place them in a saucepan with cold, salted water to cover. Bring to a boil and cook for 10 to 15 minutes, until the potatoes are tender but not mushy.

Drain the potatoes and let them rest until cool enough to handle. Dice the potatoes into ½-inch cubes and place in a medium bowl.

Heat the ham in a small sauté pan over medium heat. Add the ham, dill, sour cream, cottage cheese, and Danish blue cheese to the potatoes, tossing lightly. Season with salt and pepper to taste. Sprinkle the green onions on top. Serve immediately.

Makes 4 to 6 servings.

Scallop Ravioli

In 1992, I was able to travel outside of Alaska and eat in some very fine restaurants in the Lower 48 as well as in Europe. It seemed that everywhere I went, there was a signature ravioli dish on the menu. Here's mine.

2 tablespoons unsalted butter

Half a medium onion, peeled and finely chopped

1 pound bay scallops, minced

¼ cup ricotta cheese

1 egg yolk

2 tablespoons shredded Parmesan cheese

¼ cup finely chopped walnuts

Salt and freshly ground pepper to taste

1 pound Fresh Egg Pasta dough (see page 129)

2 quarts homemade or canned chicken stock

Red Pepper Sauce (see page 206)

Melt the butter in a large, heavy skillet over medium heat. Add the onion and cook until softened, stirring occasionally, about 8 minutes. Mix in the scallops and stir until heated through. Remove from heat. Mix in ricotta, egg yolk, Parmesan cheese, and walnuts. Season with salt and pepper. Cool the filling completely.

Roll out the pasta dough, either by hand or with a pasta machine, as thin as possible without tearing the dough. Cut into 4-inch squares. Brush the edges with cold water. Place a heaping tablespoon of the scallop filling in the center of each square. Fold the squares in half, forming rectangles; press the edges together to seal.

Bring the stock to a boil in a large pot over medium heat. Season with salt. Gently drop in the ravioli. Reduce the heat and simmer until the ravioli are just tender but still al dente, about 8 minutes. Spoon 2 tablespoons (or more) of the Red Pepper Sauce onto a plate. Place 2 ravioli on the sauce. Repeat with remaining ravioli on individual plates. Serve warm.

Makes 6 to 8 servings.

Braised Red Cabbage with Blueberries and Bacon

The color of this dish is striking—the purple of the red cabbage combined with the blue of the berries. The pairing of bacon and blueberries is what first attracted me to this unusual combination. Serve this as an accompaniment to pork or game dishes.

6 slices bacon

3 tablespoons unsalted butter

1 red onion, peeled and thinly sliced

½ pound domestic mushrooms, chopped

1 clove garlic, peeled and minced

1 head red cabbage, finely shredded

¼ cup red wine

¼ cup homemade or canned chicken stock

Salt and freshly ground pepper to taste

1 cup blueberries, fresh or frozen, thawed, and drained

Fry the bacon in a large skillet until crisp. Set aside the bacon. Drain and discard all but 2 tablespoons of the fat from the skillet. Return to heat and add the butter. Add the onion and sauté until lightly browned. Add the mushrooms and sauté for 5 minutes, or until they begin to release their liquid. Add the garlic, shredded cabbage, red wine, and chicken stock. Season with salt and pepper to taste.

Cover the skillet and cook over low heat for 20 to 30 minutes, until the cabbage is tender and the liquid is absorbed. Crumble the reserved bacon. Add the blueberries and bacon to the cabbage mixture and serve warm.

Makes 4 to 6 servings.

Eggplant Caviar

We can't grow eggplant very easily in Alaska. It grows in our greenhouse but attracts whiteflies like crazy. Since we grow everything at Riversong without chemicals, we have a constant battle. I love eggplant nonetheless, and buy it in any size, shape, and color I can find. Serve this dish as an appetizer or an accompaniment to a first course.

1 medium eggplant,
    unpeeled
1 medium onion, unpeeled
1 large tomato, peeled,
    seeded, and finely
    chopped
1 clove garlic, peeled and
    minced
Salt and freshly ground
    pepper to taste
1 tablespoon fresh lemon
    juice
⅛ teaspoon ground cumin
1 tablespoon olive oil
Crackers, minced hard-
    cooked eggs, and lemon
    wedges, as
    accompaniments

Preheat the oven to 350 degrees Fahrenheit. Place the eggplant and onion in a baking dish. Bake until the vegetables are soft (turn the eggplant occasionally), about 40 minutes.

Peel the onion and mince fine. Halve the eggplant lengthwise. Sprinkle the eggplant lightly with salt, place it cut side down in a strainer, and drain for 10 minutes.

Peel the eggplant and discard any clusters of seeds. Mince the eggplant flesh and place in a medium bowl. Add the onion, tomato, and garlic to the eggplant and mix thoroughly. Season with salt and pepper to taste. Mix in the lemon juice and cumin. Stir in the olive oil. Serve on a plate with crackers, minced hard-cooked eggs, and lemon wedges, all at room temperature.

Makes 2 servings.

Pacific Paella

This seafood medley combines Asian and Mediterranean flavors with sumptuous Alaska seafood. I prefer to use Thai jasmine rice, even in a Spanish dish with Alaska seafood. The jasmine rice has rough edges to the kernels, which makes it hold sauces well.

¼ cup dry white wine

½ teaspoon saffron threads (optional)

2 teaspoons unsalted butter

1 cup finely chopped onion

2 cloves garlic, peeled and minced

1 cup thinly sliced bell peppers (red, green, and yellow)

3 cups Thai jasmine rice, or other rice

1½ cups peeled, seeded, and coarsely chopped tomatoes

6 cups homemade or canned fish stock

¼ cup chopped fresh basil

¼ teaspoon Asian hot chili oil

1 pound bay scallops

1 pound Alaska spot shrimp

½ pound Alaska halibut

1 tablespoon fresh lemon juice

Heat the wine in a small, heavy saucepan. Add the saffron and remove from the heat. Let stand for 15 minutes.

Melt the butter in a large, heavy skillet over medium heat. Add the onion, garlic, and bell peppers. Sauté until the onion has softened, about 10 minutes. Add the rice and stir. Sauté the rice until the grains are coated with the butter. Add the tomatoes, stock, basil, hot chili oil, and the wine-saffron mixture. Bring to a boil. Reduce the heat, cover, and simmer for 20 minutes.

Add the seafood to the rice and stir well, without disturbing the rice layer on the bottom of the pan. Cover the skillet and simmer the rice over medium heat an additional 10 minutes. Sprinkle the lemon juice over the top. Serve immediately, giving your favorite diner the crusty rice from the bottom of the pan.

Makes 8 to 10 servings.

Broiled Salmon in a Horseradish Ginger Crust

The crust on this fish also works well for chicken and game birds. We make a soy sauce–sake broth to serve alongside: combine two parts fish stock to one part soy sauce, with sake added to taste, then boil the mixture until reduced by half.

3 cups fine fresh sourdough
    bread crumbs
1 cup unsalted butter
⅓ cup grated fresh
    horseradish
¼ cup grated fresh ginger
Salt and freshly ground
    white pepper to taste
8 salmon fillets (6 ounces
    each)

Preheat the broiler. Grease a baking sheet. Combine the bread crumbs, butter, horseradish, and ginger in a food processor, working it into a smooth paste. Season with salt and pepper to taste. Spread some of the paste on top of each fillet. Place the fillets on a greased baking sheet. Broil the fish at least 2 inches from the heat source until the crust is golden brown, about 10 minutes. Serve hot.

Makes 8 servings.

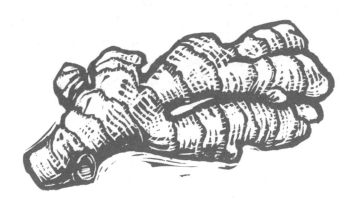

Salmon Roulades

We serve this appetizer at the bar with a creamy mustard sauce. But you could serve several roulades along with a Danish cucumber salad as a first course.

1 salmon fillet (1½ pounds)
Salt and freshly ground
  white pepper to taste
1 cup fresh cilantro
  (coriander) leaves
1 clove garlic, peeled and
  minced
4½ tablespoons olive oil
¼ cup shredded Parmesan
  cheese
1 cup fresh sourdough bread
  crumbs
¼ cup canola oil

Slice the fillet into 16 thin slices, cutting on the bias. If you are using a huge king salmon fillet, as we often do, cut the slices in half as well. Sprinkle the salmon slices with salt and pepper to taste.

In a food processor, puree the cilantro, garlic, olive oil, and Parmesan cheese to a paste. Spread the surface of one salmon slice with a thin layer of the cilantro mixture. Roll up tightly and secure with a toothpick, if necessary. Repeat with the remaining salmon slices. Chill until ready to cook.

Roll the salmon roulades in the bread crumbs to coat lightly. Heat a small amount of oil in a skillet. Sauté the roulades until browned, about 1 minute on each side. Serve on a large platter.

Makes 16 appetizers, or 4 first-course servings.

Seafood Brown Rice Fritters with Herbs

I use perilla, or shiso, in this recipe, but you can use basil or any other aromatic herb. Perilla, a cousin to basil, is the most popular herb used in Japan. Salmon works well as a substitute for halibut. Serve with Riversong Red Pepper Relish (see page 209).

1 cup cooked brown rice
1 cup cooked wild rice
1 cup cooked, flaked halibut
½ cup finely minced onion
2 tablespoons all-purpose
    flour
1 teaspoon baking powder
2 tablespoons shredded
    Parmesan cheese
2 large eggs
½ cup shredded fresh perilla
    or basil, or 1 tablespoon
    dried shiso
Salt and freshly ground
    pepper to taste
Canola oil for frying

In a medium bowl, combine thoroughly the rices, halibut, and onion. Sprinkle the flour, baking powder, and cheese over the mixture. Beat the eggs in a small bowl and stir into the rice mixture. Add the perilla or basil and season with salt and pepper.

Heat a small amount of oil on a griddle or in a wide skillet. Drop about 2 tablespoons of the rice mixture onto the hot griddle. Press the top down slightly to flatten. Cook for 2 minutes on each side, or until the rice is golden brown. Repeat with the remaining rice mixture. Serve hot.

Makes 12 fritters.

Berries by the Garden Gate

Cranberries—We have wild cranberries growing in the yard. The berries are tart and make a beautiful red juice. We use cranberries in sauces both savory and sweet.

Black currants—I planted Swedish black currant bushes at the entrance to the garden. We got them from the state of Alaska's agricultural experimental program and they have been thriving ever since. The bushes are prolific producers, and we use the berries for juices, jellies, and sauces.

Red currants—Red currants grow wild all through the woods surrounding the lodge. They hang like jewels hidden underneath their leaves. One heavy rain will knock the currants off the bush, so we watch carefully for the right time to pick them. We make red currant jellies, sauces for meats and game, and red currant syrup, and bake the currants into muffins and nut breads. I freeze currants for winter by spreading the washed berries on a baking sheet, freezing them individually, and then packaging and refreezing them.

Raspberries—Red raspberry bushes are everywhere in our part of Alaska. Raspberries make the best fruit leather—the girls make a puree of the fruit with sugar added, then spread it onto plastic wrap in a thin layer. The fruit leather dries in the greenhouse for a few days, then the girls roll it up and eat it for snacks.

Blueberry Buckle

When my sisters Katherine and Jami were babies, they loved to eat blueberry buckle. Although they are grown women now, I still think of the delight on their faces when I used to serve this to them. This is an old-fashioned dessert that can be served at lunch or dinner.

¾ cup cold unsalted butter
1 cup sugar
1 egg
2¾ cups all-purpose flour
2 teaspoons baking powder
½ teaspoon salt
½ cup milk
2 cups fresh blueberries
2 teaspoons lemon juice
½ teaspoon ground
　　cardamom
½ cup chopped pecans

Preheat the oven to 350 degrees Fahrenheit. Grease and flour a 9-by-9-by-2-inch baking pan. Cream together ½ cup of the butter and ½ cup of the sugar until fluffy. Add the egg and continue to beat until blended.

Sift 2 cups of the flour with the baking powder and salt. Add the flour mixture to the butter mixture, alternating with the milk. Pour the batter into the prepared pan. Toss the blueberries lightly in ¼ cup flour to prevent them from sinking in the batter. Sprinkle the blueberries and lemon juice on top of the batter.

Combine the remaining ½ cup sugar, ½ cup flour, ¼ cup butter, cardamom, and chopped pecans together in a food processor or mixer until crumbly. Sprinkle the nut mixture over the blueberries. Bake on the center rack of the oven for 1 hour, or until a toothpick inserted in the center comes out clean. Cut into squares and serve warm.

Makes 8 to 10 servings.

White Chocolate Rose Petal Tart with Red Currants

This tart is easy to complete in Alaska because there are so many wild rosebushes. Don't use petals from rosebushes that have been treated with pesticides.

1 cup fresh red currants
½ cup crème de cassis or cranberry liqueur
Pastry for a 9-inch single-crust flaky pie shell (see "Two Kinds of Pie Crust" on pages 47 and 48)
⅓ cup sugar
¼ cup all-purpose flour
1 cup milk
3 egg yolks
6 ounces white chocolate, chopped
1 teaspoon vanilla extract
¼ cup red currant jelly
1 cup fresh rose petals

Preheat the oven to 425 degrees Fahrenheit. Soak the currants in the liqueur. Line a 9-inch tart pan with a removable bottom with the pastry and trim off any excess. Prick the pastry with a small fork to allow steam to escape. Bake for 10 to 12 minutes. The pastry will be light golden in color. Cool on a wire rack.

Combine the sugar, flour, and milk in a heavy medium saucepan. Add the egg yolks and mix well. Bring to a boil over medium heat. Reduce the heat and cook until thick and smooth. Remove from heat. Add the white chocolate and vanilla. Stir until smooth. Cover with plastic wrap and chill for 1 hour.

Remove the tart shell from the pan. Heat the jelly in a small saucepan. Spread over the tart shell. Spoon the white chocolate mixture into the tart shell, smoothing the top with a wide rubber spatula. Chill the tart for 1 to 2 hours. Before serving, arrange the drained red currants on top of the tart and sprinkle with the rose petals.

Makes 8 servings.

Autumn

The Harvest Kitchen

One of my favorite seasons at Riversong is that splendid sliver of time between summer's end and the first snowfall. It gets a little windy then. Gold and scarlet leaves whirl and fly about. Grouse and ptarmigan grace the grounds around the lodge and squirrels skitter overhead. Everything seems to whisper loudly, "Prepare for the winter. It's coming."

We aren't much different from the other creatures that stay and lay in for the cold and dark ahead. We neither fly south nor migrate to warmer climes. We put the boats away high and dry, and convert one of the guest cabins to a warehouse for the mountains of hip waders and fishing rods that won't be needed again until the next summer.

The summer's garden is gone. The carrots are pulled and the potatoes are dried in the last days of warm sun. All the peas and berries have come in. The last of the flowers are drying on racks in the greenhouse. When the petals are dry, they'll be added to the big jar of potpourri on top of the piano. Sometimes guests ask to take a little bit of the potpourri home with them, which delights me.

In the kitchen, windows fog from the combination of cold air outside and the perpetual kettle of water on the stove, for sterilizing the row upon row of glass jars soon to be filled. There isn't too much that hasn't been "put by" in the Riversong kitchen over the years. From fresh beet relish to rose hip catsup, we view everything edible that grows past August as fair game for the preserving pot.

The fall ritual of canning and preserving can last several weeks. I love those days, as it begins to get dark again. Wood smoke curling in the crisp fall air seems to make all thoughts turn homeward to the indoors. Bright lights shining through the cabin windows invite people inside. The last of the season's guests fly-fish for rainbow trout and arctic grayling. A glass of red wine shared next to the wood stove begins the evening of fishing tales.

Relishes and chutneys, jams and jellies, savories and sweets begin to line the pantry. Mountains of clean white towels wait to receive hot glass jars from the boiling baths. Cookbooks lie open for inspiration. Sometimes we can afford to buy a case or two of fancy red peppers to add to the relishes. I can never seem to grow more than a small handful of bell peppers by season's end, and that's if the whiteflies don't get them first. Red peppers combined with onions from the garden sliced paper-thin, red wine vinegar, Thai hot peppers from the greenhouse, and a little honey are all simmered together into a thick, chunky sauce that goes well on anything. Red pepper relish is something that no one should have to face the winter without.

We make chutneys out of nearly everything: peppers, beets, onions, and many of the fruits we grow. The combination of savory bites with sweet undertones makes simple meals something special. A bowl of moose meat stew, thick with vegetables, served on a bed of hot white rice with a dollop of spicy chutney is a familiar dish in our home.

I've always had a fantasy of stocking the pantry solely with foods from our own garden. I've never gotten that far, and it seems that the cans of stewed tomatoes will always be from somewhere else, given the difficulty I have growing them. It makes me feel good, though, when someone asks about the pickled snow peas or the spicy rhubarb chutney on the moose meat stew, those special touches that come from our own harvest kitchen.

Green and Red Tomato Relish

The tomatoes we grow have names like "Siberian" and "Subarctic Maxi," developed for the Alaska climate. We grow them in the greenhouse, outside on protected mounds with plastic covers, or any way that we can think of. At the end of the season, we always have green tomatoes that we seem to use up quicker than the ripe ones!

4 pounds green tomatoes
(about 16), cored and
chopped

4 pounds ripe red tomatoes
(about 16), cored and
chopped

2 green bell peppers, halved,
seeded, and chopped

2 red bell peppers, halved,
seeded, and chopped

2 yellow bell peppers,
halved, seeded, and
chopped

1 cucumber, chopped

3 cups chopped onion

1 cup salt

6 cups cider vinegar

6 cups light brown sugar

1 teaspoon ground
cardamom

1 tablespoon mustard seed

1 tablespoon freshly ground
pepper

Combine the tomatoes, peppers, cucumber, and onion in a large bowl. Sprinkle with salt. Line a colander with cheesecloth. Place the tomato mixture in the colander and let it drain for 12 to 24 hours in a cool place.

Combine the vegetables with the vinegar, brown sugar, cardamom, mustard seeds, and pepper in a heavy, nonaluminum pot. Bring to a boil, then reduce heat and simmer, stirring occasionally, until thick, about 30 minutes. Spoon into hot, sterilized pint jars, leaving ½-inch headspace. Adjust the lids and process in a boiling-water canner for 5 minutes.

Makes 6 to 8 pints.

A Primer on Preserving

The canning recipes in this book use the boiling-water bath method. This method uses a large stockpot or boiling-water canner to process, or boil, jars of sealed food for a recommended length of time.

Clean, Mason-type, threaded glass jars with self-sealing lids are recommended.

To sterilize empty jars, put enough jars to fit comfortably right side up in a boiling-water canner. Fill the canner and the jars with hot water to at least 1 inch above the tops of the jars. Boil for 10 minutes. Remove with tongs or a jar lifter, drain the hot sterilized jars, and place on a clean, dry towel. Save the hot water in the canner for processing the filled jars.

Fill the jars with the food to be processed. Both food and jars should be hot. Add the lids, and tighten. The unfilled space above the food in a jar and below its lid is called the headspace. The headspace will vary with each recipe.

Follow these steps for successful boiling-water canning: Fill the canner halfway with water and preheat the water to 180 degrees Fahrenheit. Load the filled jars, fitted with lids, into the canner. The water level should be 1 inch above the jar tops. Add more boiling water as needed. Place the lid on the canner and lower the heat to maintain a slow boil. Process the jars for the recommended time (each recipe varies). Turn off the heat and remove the canner lid. Remove the jars and place them on a clean, dry towel to cool at room temperature.

Check the seals on the jars, following the jar manufacturer's directions. If you are using two-part screw-type lids, the center of the lid will be down and will not move when pressed.

Crab Apple Jelly

We don't have any crab apple trees at the lodge, but the yard at our Anchorage office gives us all the crab apples we could ever want.

4 pounds fresh crab apples
4 cups water
4 cups sugar

Wash, stem, and quarter the crab apples. Place them into a large pot with the water. Bring to a boil over high heat. Reduce the heat to medium and simmer for 30 minutes, stirring occasionally to prevent scorching. When the fruit is tender, strain through a colander, then through a double layer of cheesecloth. Allow the juice to drip through without pressing the fruit, which will make the jelly cloudy. You should have 4 cups of clear juice.

Combine the juice and sugar in a medium saucepan and heat until boiling. Stir until the sugar is dissolved. Boil over high heat until the jelly forms a sheet when dripped from the edge of a cool metal spoon.

Remove from the heat and quickly skim off any foam. Fill hot, sterile half-pint jars with the jelly, leaving ¼-inch headspace. Adjust the lids and process in a boiling-water canner for 5 minutes.

Makes 2 pints.

Rhubarb Chutney

Rhubarb abounds in the garden—it's the first plant to come up in the spring and the last to die back. Our rhubarb plants are more than ten years old and have survived 60-below winters. The color of cooked rhubarb is a little bland, so we add the juice from beets to perk it up.

6 cups rhubarb, diced
2 cups tart green apples (such as Granny Smith), peeled, cored, and shredded
2 cups coarsely chopped red onions
1½ cups dried currants
4 cloves garlic, peeled and minced
2 tablespoons minced fresh ginger
½ teaspoon red pepper flakes
2 cups light brown sugar
1 teaspoon ground coriander
1 teaspoon ground allspice
1 tablespoon pickling salt
2 teaspoons mustard seed
¼ teaspoon ground cloves
1 cup juice from red beets
2 cups red wine vinegar
¼ cup honey

Combine all ingredients except the red wine vinegar and honey in a large saucepan. Bring the mixture to a boil, reduce the heat, and simmer for 30 minutes. Add the vinegar and honey. Continue to cook over medium heat, stirring frequently, until the mixture is thick, about 30 minutes.

Ladle the chutney into hot, sterilized pint jars, leaving ¼-inch headspace at the top. Adjust the lids and process for 15 minutes in a boiling-water canner.

Makes 2 quarts.

Rose Hip Catsup

We went through a catsup phase for a while. We made mushroom catsup, berry catsup, you name it. The yard is full of rose hips in the fall, and I love making this aromatic condiment. It's delicious used as a marinade for vegetables. Pick the rose hips when they are soft and slightly mushy. Some people say they are best after the first frost. Don't use rose hips from bushes that have been treated with pesticides.

1 whole garlic bulb
Olive oil
1 quart rose hips
2 cups cider vinegar
2 cups sugar
1 teaspoon freshly ground
  pepper
½ teaspoon salt
¼ teaspoon hot pepper sauce
½ teaspoon dry mustard
½ teaspoon ground cloves

Preheat the oven to 350 degrees Fahrenheit. Roast the garlic by cutting off the tops of the cloves and loosening the sides. Place the garlic in foil, pour a little olive oil over the top, and cover with additional foil. Bake for 50 minutes or until the garlic is soft. Remove the garlic from the cloves by squeezing gently. Mash the garlic in a small bowl and set aside.

Clean the rose hips, removing the stem ends, and place them in a saucepan. Add enough cold water to just cover the rose hips, and bring to a boil. Simmer for 15 minutes or until soft. Strain the rose hips through a sieve to eliminate any seeds. Return the rose hip pulp to the saucepan and add the remaining ingredients. Simmer over medium heat until the mixture is thick, about 30 minutes. Pour the catsup into hot, sterilized pint jars, leaving ¼-inch headspace. Adjust the lids and process in a boiling-water canner for 15 minutes.

Makes 2 pints.

Sorrel Ginger Jelly

Sorrel is one of those wonderful herbs that can withstand our 40-below winters and still come up every spring with as much vigor as ever. Use this sorrel jelly as a condiment with game or pork.

4 cups fresh sorrel leaves
4 cups water
1 teaspoon lemon juice
2 whole cardamom pods,
 crushed
1-inch piece of fresh ginger,
 peeled and sliced
2 to 4 cups sugar
3 ounces liquid pectin

Place the sorrel in a large saucepan with the water. Add the lemon juice, cardamom, and ginger. Cover and allow to simmer for 20 to 30 minutes.

Strain the liquid through a fine-mesh sieve or double-layer cheesecloth and measure the volume of liquid. Add 2 cups of sugar for every 2 cups of liquid and place in a medium saucepan. Bring the mixture to a boil. Immediately add the liquid pectin and return to a hard boil for 1 minute. Remove from heat and skim any foam from the surface of the jelly. Pour into hot, sterilized half-pint jars, leaving ¼-inch headspace. Adjust the lids and process in a boiling-water canner for 5 minutes.

Makes 4 half-pint jars.

Fresh Beet Relish

Beets make a delicious relish. Add zucchini and you have an Alaskan condiment. Beet relish is good alongside almost anything.

5 large beets, peeled and minced
1 large red onion, peeled and minced
1 cup minced zucchini
3 tablespoons minced fresh ginger
1 cup Alaska fireweed, or other, honey
2 cups rice wine vinegar
1 teaspoon dried red pepper flakes

Place all ingredients in a large, heavy saucepan over medium heat. Bring to a boil. Reduce the heat and simmer for 20 minutes. Remove from heat and immediately pour the mixture into hot, sterilized pint jars, leaving ¼-inch headspace. Adjust the lids and process in a boiling-water canner for 30 minutes.

Makes 2 pints.

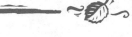

Red Pepper Sauce

I use this basic sauce for meats, fish, and pasta. Make it thick or thin as desired.

4 red bell peppers, halved,
deveined, seeded, and
chopped
⅓ cup olive oil
About ¼ cup heavy cream

Place the peppers and oil in a medium saucepan over medium heat. Simmer the peppers in the oil for 20 to 30 minutes, or until they are very soft. Puree the peppers in a food processor. Add the cream to the bell peppers, a little at a time, until the sauce is the desired consistency and color. The sauce can be frozen up to 6 months by omitting the cream until just prior to use. Serve the sauce warm.

Makes 2½ cups.

Cranberry-Currant-Walnut Sauce

Use this sauce for fish as well as game, or perhaps just as a condiment with a bowl of brown rice.

1 pound fresh cranberries
1 cup sugar
1 cup red currant jelly
1 cup orange juice
1 cup finely chopped
* walnuts*

Combine the washed cranberries with the sugar, jelly, and orange juice in a large saucepan. Bring to a boil, then reduce the heat and simmer, uncovered, for 20 minutes, skimming off any foam that collects. Remove from the heat and stir in the walnuts. The sauce will keep for 1 week, refrigerated.

Makes 6 cups.

Alaska Mixed Berry Fruit Jellies

Serve a small tray of these elegant treats on the porch in the summer with a tall glass of freshly squeezed lemonade.

2 pounds (8 cups) mixed berries (such as currants, blackberries, and raspberries)
1¼ cups granulated sugar
1 tablespoon liquid pectin
About ½ cup granulated sugar or confectioner's sugar for dusting

Pick over the berries, removing any stems or blemished berries. Puree the berries in a food processor. Place the berry puree into a medium, wide saucepan, bring to a boil, reduce the heat, and simmer for 10 to 15 minutes, or until the fruit is soft. Strain the fruit through a fine-mesh sieve into a clean medium saucepan. There should be approximately 2 cups of puree. Add the granulated sugar and the pectin to the puree. Bring the puree to a boil over medium heat, stirring frequently. Continue to stir until the mixture is thick, about 25 to 30 minutes.

Line a rectangular 9-by-13-by-2-inch baking dish with plastic wrap. Pour the fruit paste into the pan, smooth the surface, cover loosely and let stand overnight.

Remove the fruit paste from the pan onto a clean surface. Coat the paste with sugar. Cut the slab into 1-inch squares, or cut out into shapes with small cookie cutters. Dry the jellies on a wire rack for several hours before serving.

Makes about 42 (1-inch) squares.

Riversong Red Pepper Relish

This is the condiment that I couldn't face winter without. Try it on stew, burgers, grilled fish, or pasta.

4 cups red bell peppers, halved, seeded, deveined, and minced
2 cups minced red onion
2 cups red wine vinegar
1 small Thai or other hot pepper, seeded and minced
1 tablespoon minced fresh ginger
1 cup honey
1½ cups light brown sugar

Combine all the ingredients except the honey and sugar in a large saucepan. Bring the mixture to a boil over medium heat. Reduce the heat and simmer until the peppers and onions are soft, about 10 minutes. Add the honey and sugar.

Continue to simmer, stirring often, until the peppers and onions are translucent and the mixture is thick, about 30 minutes. Ladle the relish into hot, sterilized half-pint jars, leaving ¼-inch headspace. Adjust the lids and process in a boiling-water bath for 10 minutes.

Makes 5 cups.

Reflections from Seasons Past

There's a wonderful travel group in Anchorage called the Alaska Prospectors Society. Adventurers of all ages get together once a month to listen to a speaker tell of a recent hiking trip or gold panning expedition. At one gathering Carl and I were asked to speak about our lives at Riversong Lodge.

We showed slides of our home and talked about the challenges of our early years at the lodge. We told stories about the bear peeking in through the window, about barging our piano out to the lodge on a river boat, and about how we home-school our children.

We brought some smoked salmon and wild berry jam to serve as a sampling of the abundance nature provides for us. It was the first time anyone had asked us to tell our story, and our exuberance quickly filled the hour.

At the end of the evening, I was gathering the plates and the remainders of the food we had set out when an old man walked up to me. He was very tall and moved slowly.

"You know, I was in your neighborhood when I was younger," he said, bending down slightly. I set the dishes down on the table and looked into his crystal blue eyes.

"It was in 1913," he began, "and we were traveling up the river with a mule team to our gold camp. One of the fellows in our party fell through the ice there on the Yentna River and we never found him."

I caught my breath in excitement to meet such a man. Long before I was even born, he had been a small part of the place that I claim as my own. I felt humbled.

What a journey it must have been to travel overland to Lake Creek in the early 1900s. I can imagine this man, a young kid in a plaid shirt and heavy leather boots, looking for his fortune, everything ahead of him. Mules laden with supplies, sinking in the snow, campfires hastily built before nightfall, heavy canvas tents hoisted up—these difficulties and more the pioneers accepted. In my life, I think it is a notable task to unload supplies from a floatplane to get them to the lodge.

I was too preoccupied about the time and the babysitter to linger longer with the man. In the glow of our evening, I didn't ask his name or address.

A few weeks later, I received a small envelope with a recipe for clover wine from the man. The recipe card was now brown with age. On the back a small notation read, "Given to Carl Berlin on 5/14/29."

I hope when I am an old woman I'll meet a young couple who are excited to share their stories of life on the Yentna River. I'll listen to them carefully and respectfully and then I'll send them a very special recipe for clover wine. (See Carl Berlin's Clover Wine, page 225.)

Spicy Rabbit Stew

We attempt to raise rabbits for the kitchen, but more bears and coyotes enjoy them than we do. Even the wild animals know the food is special at Riversong. Serve this stew with wide, buttery egg noodles, loads of Sweet Potato Corn Bread (see page 223), and a dollop of Cranberry-Currant-Walnut Sauce (see page 207).

1 medium onion, peeled, thinly sliced, and separated into rings
1 clove garlic, peeled and minced
2 tablespoons unsalted butter
1 tablespoon olive oil
1 rabbit (2½ pounds), cut up
½ cup all-purpose flour
Salt and freshly ground pepper to taste
4 whole cloves
¼ teaspoon ground allspice
¼ teaspoon ground cumin
2 tablespoons brown sugar
1½ cups dry red wine
1½ cups homemade or canned beef stock
¼ cup red currant jelly
Juice of 1 lemon
2 tablespoons red wine vinegar
½ cup cranberries

In a skillet large enough to hold the rabbit, sauté the onion and garlic in the butter and olive oil over medium heat for 4 to 5 minutes, until softened.

Dredge the rabbit in the flour. Add the rabbit to the skillet and brown on all sides. Add salt and pepper to taste. Add the cloves, allspice, ground cumin, and brown sugar. Gradually add the wine, beef stock, red currant jelly, lemon juice, and vinegar. Cover the skillet and simmer for 1 hour, or until the rabbit is tender. Add the cranberries. Simmer for another 10 minutes, covered.

Makes 4 servings.

Smoked Duck Potato Galette

We make this dish when we have smoked duck left over from the night before. A dollop of sour cream brings out the flavor of the cabbage. A sauce made from heated red currant jelly and a little vinegar goes well with this galette.

8 large potatoes, peeled
6 tablespoons unsalted
    butter
1 small head green cabbage
Salt and freshly ground
    pepper to taste
2 pounds smoked duck
    meat, shredded (see
    page 75)

Julienne the potatoes (cut into matchstick strips) with a food processor or by hand. In a large, nonstick skillet, melt 3 tablespoons of the butter. Arrange two-thirds of the julienned potatoes in a circular pattern on the bottom of the skillet. Season with salt to taste. Cook over medium heat for 10 minutes.

Shred the cabbage. In a separate skillet, melt the remaining 3 tablespoons butter. Add the cabbage and cook over medium heat for 5 minutes, or until the cabbage has softened and is slightly translucent. Add the remaining potatoes and continue to cook without browning for an additional 5 minutes. Season with salt and pepper to taste.

Place the shredded duck meat over the julienned potatoes in the first pan. Spread the cabbage-potato mixture on top of the meat and press down slightly with the back of a spatula or spoon. Cook the potatoes over medium heat for 5 to 7 minutes. Gently slide the potatoes out of the skillet onto a large plate, then invert the plate over the skillet to turn the potatoes over. Cook for an additional 5 to 7 minutes, or until the potatoes are golden brown. Slice into wedges and serve, julienned potato side up.

Makes 4 servings.

Apple-Cranberry Cannoli

This dessert can be adapted many different ways. Once you get the hang of working with phyllo dough, these sweet, crisp rolls take only a minute to assemble. Serve hot with a berry sauce or with ice cream.

PASTRY CREAM:
2 cups heavy cream
¼ cup sugar
4 egg yolks

CANNOLI:
2 cups unsalted butter,
*   melted*
1 cup granulated sugar
5 large apples, peeled, cored,
*   and shredded*
1 cup finely chopped
*   cranberries*
½ cup finely chopped and
*   pan-toasted walnuts*
20 sheets phyllo dough
Powdered sugar, as needed

To make the pastry cream, combine the heavy cream and 2 tablespoons of the sugar in a saucepan. Scald the cream and remove from heat. Beat the remaining 2 tablespoons sugar and the egg yolks in a mixer until light and fluffy. Add the hot cream to the yolks in a steady stream, whisking constantly. Place the mixture into the top of a double boiler. Simmer over medium-low heat, whisking constantly, until thick, but don't bring the mixture to a boil. When the pastry cream is thick enough to coat a spoon, remove from heat, strain through a fine mesh into a small, clean bowl to remove any lumps, and cool the cream over a larger bowl filled with ice.

To make the cannoli, preheat the oven to 375 degrees Fahrenheit. Grease a baking sheet. Place 1 cup of the melted butter in a large skillet and add sugar. Add the apples and cook over low heat until tender, about 5 minutes. Add the cranberries and nuts. Remove from heat and let cool.

Place one phyllo sheet on a work surface (keep remaining sheets covered). Brush the sheet with some of the remaining melted butter. Top the buttered phyllo sheet with a new sheet. Butter the second sheet. Repeat the process with three more phyllo sheets. Dust lightly with powdered sugar. Spread 3 tablespoons of pastry cream

continued on next page

on the buttered phyllo, leaving a ½-inch border. Add 3 tablespoons of the apple-cranberry mixture. Roll the long edge of the phyllo up ½ inch lengthwise, then turn the sides in ½ inch (similar to folding a burrito). Roll the phyllo up lengthwise and brush with butter to seal the edges. Repeat with remaining sheets of phyllo. Place the cannoli on the baking sheet. Bake until the cannoli are brown and crisp, about 15 to 20 minutes.

Makes 4 cannoli.

Pumpkin Cake in a Jar

I wrote a food column in *ALASKA* magazine for two years, and of all the recipes we published, this one elicited more letters and comments than any other. The pumpkin cake is baked in a jar, ready to give as a gift or include in a picnic basket.

⅔ cup vegetable shortening
2⅔ cups sugar
4 eggs
2 cups pureed fresh or
    canned pumpkin
⅔ cup water
3⅓ cups all-purpose flour
½ teaspoon baking powder
1½ teaspoons salt
1 teaspoon ground cloves
1 teaspoon ground allspice
1 teaspoon ground
    cinnamon
2 teaspoons baking soda
1 cup chopped walnuts

Preheat the oven to 350 degrees Fahrenheit. Grease 8 wide-mouth pint jars. Cream the shortening and the sugar together, adding the sugar slowly. Beat in the eggs, pumpkin, and water. Set aside.

Sift together the flour, baking powder, salt, cloves, allspice, cinnamon, and baking soda. Add the flour mixture to the pumpkin mixture and stir well. Stir in the nuts. Pour the batter into the prepared jars, filling them half full. Place the jars upright on a baking sheet. Bake on the center rack of the oven for about 45 minutes. The cake will rise and pull away from the sides of the jar. When the cake is done, remove one jar at a time from the oven.

While still warm, place a circle of waxed paper on top of each cake and place the lid on the jar. I don't recommend storing these cakes for any length of time, but they make unusual gifts or take-along desserts. Slide the cake out of the jar when ready to serve.

Makes 8 cakes.

Tapioca Pudding with Caramel

This dessert is like a regular tapioca pudding, but with a caramel glaze over the top. The glaze intensifies the vanilla flavor.

¾ cup sugar
Cold water
3 tablespoons quick-cooking
  tapioca
Pinch of salt
2 cups cold milk
2 eggs, separated, at room
  temperature
1 teaspoon vanilla extract

Heat ½ cup of the sugar and 3 tablespoons of the cold water in a small saucepan over medium heat until the sugar dissolves. With a moistened pastry brush, push down any sugar crystals that cling to the sides of the saucepan. Bring the sugar mixture to a boil, removing the pan from the heat just as the sugar turns golden in color. Quickly pour the syrup into a 9-inch glass pie plate, tilting the plate to coat the bottom evenly with syrup.

Stir the remaining sugar, the tapioca, and the salt in a clean, medium saucepan until blended. Gradually stir in the milk. Bring the mixture to a boil over medium heat, stirring constantly. Remove the saucepan from the heat and stir in the egg yolks and vanilla. Allow the mixture to cool slightly.

Preheat the oven to 325 degrees Fahrenheit. Beat the egg whites until stiff but not dry. Fold the whites gently into the tapioca mixture. Carefully pour the mixture into the prepared pie plate. Place the pie plate into a large baking pan; place on the center rack in the oven. Make a hot-water bath by pouring enough hot water (from a teakettle) into the baking sheet to cover halfway up the sides of the pie plate.

Bake the pudding for 20 to 25 minutes, or until the center is firm to the touch. Remove the baking pan from the oven. Remove the pudding from the hot-water bath and cool for 10 minutes.

To serve, run a sharp knife around the rim of the pudding. Place a large serving platter over the pie plate; invert the pudding onto the platter. Serve warm, spooning the caramel over each serving.

Makes 4 to 6 servings.

Danish Bear Claws

What could be better for a morning treat? Be creative and use the Danish pastry dough with a variety of different fillings and shapes.

PASTRY:
1 cup cold milk
2 packages (2 tablespoons) active dry yeast
¼ cup granulated sugar
2 eggs
5 cups all-purpose flour
2 cups cold unsalted butter

FILLING:
¾ cup all-purpose flour
½ cup firmly packed light brown sugar
¼ cup cold unsalted butter
½ cup chopped toasted almonds
2 egg yolks
Pinch of salt
1 cup pureed prunes

1 egg, beaten, for wash
½ cup grated unsweetened coconut

To make the pastry, combine the milk, yeast, granulated sugar, and eggs in a large bowl. Sift in the flour, stirring until the mixture forms a kneadable dough. Knead the dough just until it is smooth, about 3 minutes. Place the dough onto a lightly floured surface and shape into a large square.

Form the butter into a square and place it on top of the dough. Fold the dough up over the butter to form another square. With a rolling pin, roll out the dough into a rectangle about ½ inch thick. Fold the short ends of the dough over each other, with each fold one-third of the way in from the end. You will have 3 overlapping layers. The dough has now been rolled *once*. Repeat the rolling two more times. Divide the dough into 4 pieces and set aside in a cool place.

To make the filling, combine the flour and brown sugar in a small bowl. Cut in the butter with a pastry blender until the mixture resembles coarse meal. Stir in the almonds, egg yolks, and salt. Set aside.

To assemble the bear claws, line two baking sheets with parchment paper. Divide one piece of dough into fourths and roll out one piece on a lightly floured surface into a 5-inch-by-8-inch rectangle. Spread the pastry with some of the prune puree, leaving a ¼-inch margin around the edges (see drawings below). (1) Sprinkle 2 tablespoons of the filling mixture over the puree. (2) Roll up the pastry from the long end and pinch the seam to seal it. Flatten slightly and slash perpendicularly on the sealed-seam side 5 or 6 times. (3) Curve the pastry into a half-moon shape to open the slashes slightly. Place the pastry on the prepared baking sheet. Repeat with the remaining dough, placing 8 bear claws on each baking sheet. Brush with the egg wash.

Preheat the oven to 400 degrees Fahrenheit. Allow the pastries to rest at room temperature for 30 minutes. Reglaze the pastries with the egg wash. Sprinkle the coconut evenly on the tops of the bear claws. Bake on the center rack of the oven for 20 minutes. Cool on a wire rack and serve warm.

Makes 16 bear claws.

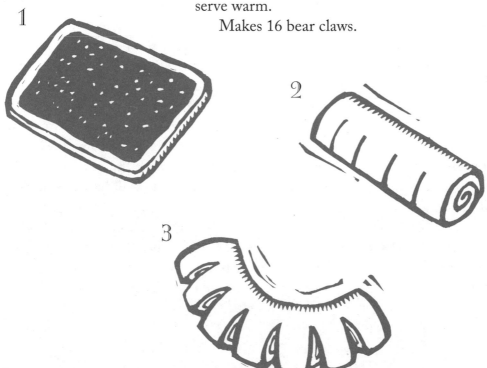

Sourdough Bread Pudding with Yukon Jack Sauce

Although Yukon Jack is a Canadian liqueur, we have adopted it as our own. This dessert is very popular at the lodge.

SOURDOUGH BREAD PUDDING:
½ cup golden raisins
2 tablespoons dark rum
1 pound day-old sourdough bread (about 8 cups), cut into 1-inch cubes
2 cups milk
2 cups heavy cream
3 eggs, beaten
2 cups granulated sugar
3 tablespoons unsalted butter, melted
2 tablespoons vanilla extract
½ teaspoon ground cinnamon

YUKON JACK SAUCE:
½ cup unsalted butter
½ cup firmly packed light brown sugar
½ cup granulated sugar
1 egg
3 tablespoons Yukon Jack liqueur

To make the pudding, soak the raisins in the rum for 20 minutes. Preheat the oven to 325 degrees Fahrenheit. Butter a 9-by-13-by-2-inch baking pan.

Place the bread cubes in a large bowl. Pour the milk and heavy cream over the bread. Let soak for 5 minutes. Whisk 3 eggs with 2 cups sugar, 3 tablespoons melted butter, vanilla, and cinnamon in a medium bowl. Pour the egg mixture over the bread. Add the raisins and rum and toss to mix. Transfer the mixture to the prepared pan. Bake on the center rack of the oven until the bread pudding is golden brown, about 1 hour.

To make the sauce, melt ½ cup butter, the brown sugar, and ½ cup granulated sugar together over low heat, stirring until the sugars are dissolved. Whisk the egg in a small bowl. Gradually whisk in some of the melted butter-sugar mixture, then return all to the saucepan. Whisk until the sauce is smooth, without boiling. Whisk in the liqueur. Spoon the warm bread pudding onto dessert plates. Spoon the sauce over the top.

Makes 8 to 12 servings.

Sweet Potato Corn Bread

This beautiful bread goes well with Spicy Rabbit Stew or Riversong Moose Stew. If you have a cast iron corn-stick pan, make bread sticks to go with a main-course salad.

2 medium sweet potatoes
  (about 1 pound), peeled
  and cut into chunks
1 cup yellow cornmeal
1 cup all-purpose flour
1 tablespoon sugar
1 tablespoon baking powder
½ teaspoon baking soda
½ teaspoon salt
¼ teaspoon ground allspice
1½ cups buttermilk
1 egg, lightly beaten
3 tablespoons unsalted
  butter

Preheat the oven to 400 degrees Fahrenheit. Boil the sweet potatoes until tender, 15 to 20 minutes. Drain thoroughly. Mash the potatoes well and place in a medium bowl.

Sift the cornmeal, flour, sugar, baking powder, baking soda, salt, and allspice together into a small bowl. Beat the buttermilk and egg into the sweet potatoes until blended.

Grease a 9-inch-square baking pan generously and heat it in the oven until sizzling, about 2 minutes. Quickly add the dry ingredients to the buttermilk mixture and stir just until blended. Pour the batter into the prepared pan.

Bake until the bread is light golden and has shrunk from the sides of the pan, about 25 minutes. Cut into squares and serve immediately.

Makes 9 to 12 squares.

Cheddar Cheese Popovers

I love to make these popovers when I am having an especially busy breakfast. They are quick and easy and everyone loves them. Steam causes the batter to rise the way it does.

1 cup all-purpose flour
¼ teaspoon salt
1 cup whole milk
⅔ cup shredded Cheddar
   cheese
1 tablespoon unsalted
   butter, melted
2 eggs

Preheat the oven to 450 degrees Fahrenheit. Generously grease the popover pans or regular muffin cups (popovers can be difficult to remove if they stick), and preheat them. Beat all the ingredients together until just smooth. Don't overbeat the mixture.

Fill the prepared pans one-half to two-thirds full. Bake on the center rack of the oven for 15 minutes. Reduce the temperature to 350 degrees Fahrenheit without opening the oven door. Bake until the popovers are firm and golden brown, 15 to 20 minutes more. Carefully remove the popovers to a linen-covered basket and serve warm with butter and jam.

Makes 8 to 12 popovers.

Carl Berlin's Clover Wine

I'm not sure whether Carl Berlin is the man who sent me this recipe, or just an early owner of the recipe card. Regardless, the faded 3-by-5-inch card is a treasure in my recipe box. Remember that this is an old recipe—wine-making techniques have become more sophisticated over the years. If you've never made wine before, I recommend that you check with a local home-brewing supplier before attempting this recipe.

1 gallon clover blossoms
1 gallon boiling water
3 pounds sugar
3 oranges, washed and
    sliced
3 lemons, washed and sliced
2 packages (2 tablespoons)
    active dry yeast

Place the clover blossoms in a large, spotlessly clean container (it must be free of bacteria). Pour the boiling water over the blossoms. Loosely cover and let stand for 3 days.

Strain the liquid, discarding the blossoms, and add the sugar, oranges, lemons, and yeast. Place the liquid in a glass or ceramic container and let it ferment at room temperature for 3 weeks. Cover the top with cheesecloth, but do not seal the container or it may explode. Strain the liquid and pour it into clean, sterilized bottles. Cap or cork the wine.

Makes 1 gallon.

Down the River

Each year in the fall, we take a float trip down Lake Creek. It takes five carefree days to travel from the river's headwaters, Chelatna Lake, back to our front door. We fly to Chelatna Lake from the lodge in a de Havilland Beaver, a large floatplane. One of my favorite parts of the trip is when the plane leaves us and lifts off the water. I feel a certain childish glee from being unreachable.

The lake is an icy-blue bowl surrounded by high mountains that are reflected in the clear, cold water. It's a place where summer is a brief kiss, perfect but elusive. Fat rainbow trout live here. One time I hooked a huge rainbow near Chelatna Lake. It leaped out of the water, skittered and arched over my head, then dove back into the icy blueness. Carl gently released the barbless hook from the fish's mouth, and with a defiant flick of the tail, my rainbow was gone.

I like to travel down Lake Creek just as fall is approaching. The night sky is visible again after the long days of summer, and the mystery of winter is about to enclose us. Berries are everywhere. I spend my camp time picking berries while Carl and the girls quietly fish. On the river, mergansers skim the water, darting from spot to spot, and wild geese fly overhead.

Along Lake Creek, in a place that is nearly hidden from view, there is a decaying trapper's cabin. I would guess it is about 100 years old. The small, one-room structure is still standing but has lost some of its original furnishings over the years. An old bunk, a rusted cook stove, and a few pots, pans, and old books are all that is left. Sometimes we make the trapper's cabin a lunch stop, staying long enough to savor the history of the area. The trapper probably hunted marten and beaver in the winter to earn enough money for the following summer and fall. He would sell the furs he trapped in Anchorage or Seattle, and eventually they would be made into fancy coats and hats. The trapper would probably be astonished to see us today, rafting to this place for recreation, laughing and playing, eating fresh fruits and vegetables from our big coolers. What would he think of us? What did he do for recreation, I wonder. Did he climb to the large open field behind the cabin and look for wild violets, or would he notice all the Queen Anne's lace that lines the path to the cabin?

The camaraderie of the campfire brings out the best in everyone on our river trips. Carly and Amanda gather wood for the fire while Carl and I organize the camp. The kitchen tent is set up and the coals are turned until just perfect. We tell tall tales late into the night, chattering lightheartedly until we fall asleep.

We have traveled down Lake Creek in good weather and in bad, with our best friends and with strangers. Our children have known it from the time they could wear a life jacket. Each time we camp along the banks or raft through the canyon, we discover something new.

Long after the float trip is over, our thoughts will return often to the glow of the campfire and to sharing a meal underneath a million stars. It's our favorite kind of family dinner together.

Eggs with Cheese

On a river trip, this breakfast can be accomplished easily on the cook stove with a covered pan.

2 tablespoons unsalted
 butter
1 tablespoon all-purpose
 flour
1 teaspoon Dijon mustard
Salt and freshly ground
 pepper to taste
½ cup milk
½ cup shredded sharp
 Cheddar cheese
6 eggs
6 slices sourdough bread,
 toasted

Preheat the oven to 325 degrees Fahrenheit. Grease an 7-by-11-by-2-inch baking dish. Melt the butter in a small saucepan over medium-low heat. Stir in the flour, mustard, salt, and pepper. Gradually add the milk. Continue cooking until the mixture is smooth and thick, stirring frequently, about 5 minutes. Add the cheese and stir until melted.

Pour the cheese sauce into the prepared dish. Carefully break the eggs into the sauce. Bake until the eggs are set, 10 to 15 minutes. Slice into 6 squares. Serve on sourdough toast, napping with the cheese sauce.

Makes 6 servings.

Skillet Garlic Potatoes

We serve these potatoes both as a breakfast dish and as a side dish for other meals. The longer the garlic cooks, the more it sweetens and mellows in flavor.

¼ cup olive oil
1 pound potatoes, scrubbed
  and cut into cubes
10 cloves garlic, peeled and
  halved
Leaves from 1 large sprig
  fresh rosemary
Salt and freshly ground
  pepper to taste

Heat the olive oil in a large, heavy skillet over high heat. Spread the potatoes over the bottom of the pan and sauté for about 10 minutes. Turn the potatoes over and add the garlic. Continue to sauté until the potatoes are golden, about 10 minutes. Add the rosemary leaves, and season with salt and pepper to taste.

Makes 6 servings.

Jesse's Cabbage Salad

Jesse McGuire has been coming to Riversong for years. One year he brought a cooler full of cabbages from his home in Oregon and made this salad for the whole lodge.

1 small head cabbage
1 package Oriental-
    flavored noodle soup mix
    (ramen)
6 green onions, chopped
½ pound cooked, flaked
    salmon
1 cup sliced almonds
¼ cup sesame seeds
⅓ cup canola oil
3 tablespoons lemon juice
1½ tablespoons sugar
Freshly ground pepper to
    taste

Shred the cabbage and place it in a large bowl. Lightly crush the noodles, reserving the soup flavoring packet. Toss the cabbage with the uncooked noodles, green onions, salmon, almonds, and sesame seeds.

Whisk the oil, lemon juice, sugar, pepper, and soup flavoring packet together in a small bowl. Drizzle the oil mixture over the salad, tossing well.

Makes 4 servings.

Vegetable Hash Baked in a Skillet

We serve this hash as a breakfast dish or as a vegetarian main dish at other meals. We modify the ingredients according to the season.

6 tablespoons unsalted butter

1 large onion, peeled and diced

2 cloves garlic, peeled and minced

1 large carrot, peeled and diced

1 large potato, diced

⅓ cup homemade or canned chicken stock

1 red bell pepper, diced into ½ inch pieces

1 cup sliced wild mushrooms

¼ cup fresh basil, finely chopped

1 egg

3 tablespoons heavy cream

Salt and freshly ground pepper to taste

½ cup grated white Cheddar cheese

Heat 3 tablespoons of the butter in a large, oven-proof skillet over medium heat. Add the onion and saute until soft, about 10 minutes. Add the garlic, carrot, potato, and chicken stock to the skillet. Cover and braise the vegetables until tender and the liquid is absorbed, 6 to 8 minutes. Remove 1 cup of the vegetable mixture and set aside. Add the red pepper, mushrooms, and basil to the skillet. Continue to cook uncovered for an additional 5 minutes, tossing the vegetables gently to mix.

Preheat the oven to 450 degrees Fahrenheit. Puree the reserved 1 cup of vegetables, the egg, and the cream in a food processor until almost smooth. Scrape into a large bowl. Add the vegetables from the skillet to the bowl. Season to taste with salt and pepper.

Heat the remaining 3 tablespoons butter in the same skillet over high heat. Add the vegetable mixture, spreading it evenly in the bottom of the skillet. Cook for 2 to 3 minutes over medium-high heat. Bake in the oven until browned, 10 to 15 minutes. Heat the broiler. Sprinkle the cheese over the hash. Broil until browned, 1 to 2 minutes. Cut the hash into wedges and serve immediately.

Makes 4 to 6 servings.

Crustless Spinach Pie

We make many different pies for lunches at the lodge. Europeans are delighted with this dish. Adapt the recipe for a river trip by preparing the pie in a large cast iron skillet over the camp stove.

1 cup finely chopped onion
1½ cups sliced wild
　mushrooms
1½ cups sliced summer
　squash (a variety of
　types, preferably)
1 clove garlic, peeled and
　minced
3 tablespoons canola oil
5 eggs
2 cups ricotta cheese
1 tablespoon fresh thyme
3 cups fresh spinach,
　blanched, drained, and
　chopped
½ cup feta cheese, crumbled
Salt and freshly ground
　pepper to taste

Preheat the oven to 350 degrees Fahrenheit. Grease a 10-inch springform pan. In a large skillet, sauté the onion, mushrooms, squash, and garlic in the oil until softened, about 10 minutes. Combine the eggs and ricotta cheese in a large bowl. Beat until well blended. Add the sautéed vegetables, thyme, spinach, and feta cheese. Season the mixture with salt and pepper. Pour into the prepared springform pan. Place on the center rack of the oven and bake for 1 hour, or until set. Serve in wedges.

Makes 8 servings.

Alder-smoked Black Cod

We have alder growing all over our property. We soak alder chips and place them on glowing coals to add a haunting, smoked flavor to fish and meats.

2 black cod steaks, 1-inch thick (about 2 pounds)
Coarse or kosher salt and fresh ground pepper
2 cups alderwood chips, soaked in water for 30 minutes

Lightly rinse the cod steaks and pat them dry. Sprinkle the cod with a light layer of salt. Cover with plastic wrap and refrigerate for 30 minutes. Start the charcoal in the grill. Lightly rinse the salt from the cod steaks; pat dry. Let stand, uncovered, for 15 minutes or until a transparent film forms on the fish. Season the steaks to taste with pepper. Drain the alderwood chips and sprinkle them over the hot coals. Place the fish on a clean, oiled grill rack 1 inch above the coals. Cover the grill and cook until the cod steaks are just done, about 10 minutes. Cut the steaks in half and serve immediately.

Makes 4 servings.

Rabbit and Reindeer Sausage Skewers

I prefer wooden skewers, but I soak them in water so they don't burn over the fire. Metal skewers always seem to impart a metallic taste. Serve this entrée with brown rice topped with shredded Cheddar cheese and a dollop of sour cream.

1 large rabbit (about 2½ pounds)
2 cups white vinegar
⅓ cup canola oil
¼ cup dried sage leaves
4 large sprigs fresh rosemary
Salt and freshly ground pepper to taste
1½ pounds Alaska reindeer sausage
1½ pounds zucchini
Olive oil, for brushing the skewers

Bone the rabbit meat and cut it into 2-inch cubes. Place the rabbit meat in a medium bowl. Add the vinegar and oil. Add ¼ cup of the sage leaves, crumbling them onto the rabbit. Remove the leaves from 2 of the rosemary sprigs and add the leaves to the marinade. Mix well, cover, and refrigerate for 6 to 12 hours. Drain the rabbit meat from the marinade. Cut the reindeer sausage into 2-inch pieces. Cut the zucchini into 2-inch pieces.

On 8-inch water-soaked skewers, alternate the marinated rabbit, zucchini, and reindeer sausage. Brush the skewers lightly with the olive oil. Remove the leaves from the remaining rosemary sprigs and sprinkle the leaves over the skewers. Grill the skewers until the rabbit meat is firm and white, about 10 minutes.

Makes 4 servings.

Sweet Potato and Reindeer Sausage Soup

This recipe has great outdoor potential. Sweet potatoes last forever, and this soup is so easy it could readily be prepared on a camp stove.

2 tablespoons canola oil

2 cloves garlic, peeled and minced

1 large onion, peeled and diced

2 medium tart green apples (such as Granny Smith), peeled, cored, and coarsely chopped

3 large sweet potatoes or yams, peeled and sliced

1 quart homemade or canned chicken stock

2 cups heavy cream

½ pound Alaska reindeer sausage

Salt and freshly ground white pepper to taste

Hot red pepper sauce to taste

Heat the oil in a large stockpot. Add the garlic and onion. Sauté over medium heat until the onion is softened, about 10 minutes. Add the apples and sweet potatoes. Stir in the stock. Cover and simmer until the vegetables are very soft, about 40 minutes.

Add the cream and stir well. Slice the reindeer sausage and add to the soup. Heat the soup until the sausage is warmed through, about 10 minutes. Stir in the salt, pepper, and hot pepper sauce to taste. Serve immediately.

Makes 4 to 6 servings.

River Cookies

These cookies combine white and dark chocolate with coconut, oats, and pecans. Carl takes big bags of them along on all his river trips. Guests, pilots, and boatmen all love them. Buy date sugar at health food stores.

1 cup all-purpose flour
1 teaspoon baking soda
1 teaspoon salt
1 cup flaked, sweetened
   coconut
½ cup rolled oats
1 cup date sugar
1 cup unsalted butter, at
   room temperature
1½ cups packed light brown
   sugar
2 teaspoons vanilla extract
2 large eggs
1 cup semisweet chocolate
   pieces
1 cup chopped pecans

Preheat the oven to 350 degrees Fahrenheit. Lightly grease a baking sheet. Process the flour, baking soda, salt, coconut, oats, and date sugar in a food processor until finely ground.

In a large bowl, cream the butter and sugar together until light. Add the vanilla. Beat in the eggs, one at a time, blending thoroughly. Add the flour mixture to the butter mixture, blending completely. Add the chocolate and nuts, stirring well. Drop tablespoons of the batter onto the prepared baking sheet, about 2 inches apart. Bake 10 to 12 minutes, or until the cookies are golden. Remove the cookies from the oven and cool completely before serving.

Makes 48 cookies.

Barbecue Sauce for Fish or Meats

It's nearly impossible not to catch fish on a Lake Creek float trip. Make this sauce at home, store it in sealable plastic bags or in a jar, and pack it for serving with freshly caught fish.

½ cup olive oil

1 small onion, finely chopped

3 cloves garlic, peeled and minced

1½ cups red bell pepper, cored, seeded, and finely chopped

1½ cups yellow bell pepper, cored, seeded, and finely chopped

1 cup finely chopped pan-toasted walnuts

⅓ cup cider vinegar

Salt and freshly ground pepper to taste

Heat the olive oil in a heavy saucepan over medium heat. Add the onion and garlic. Cook for 5 minutes, or until the onion is softened. Add the peppers. Reduce the heat and cook for about 10 minutes, or until the peppers are wilted. Stir in the walnuts, vinegar, and salt and pepper to taste. Increase the heat to high and cook for 5 minutes, or until almost all of the liquid is absorbed. The sauce will keep 1 week, refrigerated.

Makes 2 pints.

Through My Kitchen Door

Over the years, so many people have influenced my cooking that it's hard to imagine what the lodge would be like without their contributions. Employees and guests alike have come into the Riversong kitchen and prepared meals that, more than being just food, have been true celebrations of life. These moments of sharing with friends are some of the memories I most treasure.

Robert Litti is a wizened, white-haired German man who comes to our lodge year after year. He owns a small Renault bicycle and motorcycle shop in a picturesque town near the German-Swiss border and lives in rooms above his shop. Each year he brings special gifts to the kitchen from his homeland.

One year, Litti brought a *spaetzle*, or noodle, maker to the lodge. It's a hand-held press that produces wonderful round noodles from egg dough. For the entire lodge, he prepared his version of sauerbraten, a traditional German beef dish made with juniper berries and vinegar. He marinated the meat for three days in the root cellar. The braised sauerbraten was served with fresh spaetzle.

Anne Willan is the president and founder of La Varenne, the prestigious cooking school in France. I once persuaded her to conduct a culinary weekend at the lodge. And what a weekend it was! During Anne's visit, we encountered numerous cooking challenges, from power failures to airplane delays, yet the show went on. We had planned to prepare a whole salmon baked in a rich, buttery dough called *brioche*. Anne sent one of the guides out for a fresh fish, and he returned with a 40-pound king salmon, about ten times bigger than she had expected. Without missing a beat, she commanded the class to make a megabatch of brioche, and with some hard work, we managed to wrap the huge fish in dough. In the end, with Anne's special touch, the salmon turned out beautifully: the brioche was a rich, golden brown and the fish was perfectly moist inside. Who cares if we made enough to feed Napoleon's army?

Margaret Hayes, or Maggie as we call her, is an ear surgeon in Anchorage. On her rare days off, she comes to the lodge and dons an apron. She likes to make cookies and her favorite is oatmeal-raisin. Maggie also likes to do the odd jobs around the kitchen that we never seem to have time for—polishing the silver, organizing the linen shelves, and ironing tablecloths. We overwhelmed Maggie's baking ability one day when we had a group of NFL football players visiting. She baked all day and still couldn't get ahead of the demand.

Maggie's hobby in Anchorage is to haunt garage sales. Nearly every piece of tableware and linen at the lodge has been a treasured find from Maggie's diligent sleuthing.

Over the years, many extraordinary people have come through my kitchen door, and I think with joy of the ones still to arrive. The Riversong kitchen is special that way—there's always another season, always room for creativity and change. Just like the river flowing in front of the lodge, life goes on here, ever changing yet ever the same.

Robert Litti's Spaetzle

Robert's spaetzle maker sits on the kitchen shelf, always at the ready to make these delightful little noodles. Spaetzle are a traditional accompaniment to sauerbraten (see recipe on page 246).

4 cups all-purpose flour
½ cup milk
1 cup club soda
4 eggs
1 teaspoon salt
½ cup unsalted butter

Sift the flour into a bowl. Add the milk and soda water, mixing well. Add the eggs and salt, mix, and beat the dough with a wooden spoon until small bubbles form. Let the dough rest for 30 minutes.

Bring 4 quarts salted water to a boil in a large pot. If you have a spaetzle maker, press the dough through it into the boiling water. If you have a colander or sieve, grease it well and try pushing the dough through the holes. If none of these are available, cut or slice the spaetzle into 1-inch pieces into the boiling water. Bring each batch briefly to a boil, then lift the spaetzle out with a slotted spoon, drain in a colander, and chill under cold running water.

Place the spaetzle in a sauté pan over medium heat to steam off any excess moisture. Add the butter and sauté until the butter is melted and the noodles are warm.

Makes 6 to 8 servings.

Dave Wallin's Salmon Caviar

Dave Wallin is a physician from New Orleans, who once saved a goose of mine that had swallowed a fishhook. Dave brought me a salmon egg screen that makes cleaning the roe from the skein easier. The eggs drop through the screen, leaving the skein behind. We serve salmon caviar with toast points as an appetizer at the bar.

½ cup salt
2 cups water
2 cups fresh salmon eggs
1 tablespoon soy sauce
Half a lemon, cut into small
    wedges

Dissolve the salt in the water in a small bowl. Break the roe sac of the salmon eggs and empty the eggs into a large bowl. Remove as much of the membrane as possible. We have a screen with a mesh large enough for eggs to drop through, leaving the membrane behind. Gently pour the brine over the eggs and let sit for at least 1 hour.

Add the soy sauce and lemon wedges. (We place the eggs and brine in our root cellar for 3 days or more, changing the brine-soy-lemon mixture each day.) The brine firms the eggs up. Drain the eggs with a strainer and rinse gently with cold water. Remove any white particles that might remain from the sac casings. Store the eggs in the refrigerator in a clean glass jar. Caviar will keep indefinitely.

Makes 2 cups.

Adolph Frey's Pike Quenelles

Adolph Frey owns one of the few Michelin-rated two-star restaurants in Germany. He made this dish at the lodge for Carl's birthday celebration one year. Quenelles are poached fish-and-egg mounds that are traditionally made with pike.

QUENELLES:
2½ pounds pike, skinned and boned
1¼ cups water
1¼ cups all-purpose flour
2 eggs
1 cup unsalted butter
Salt and freshly ground pepper to taste
4 egg yolks

WHITE SAUCE:
1 quart homemade or canned chicken stock
1½ cups heavy cream
Salt and freshly ground pepper to taste
½ cup shredded Parmesan cheese

To make the quenelles, grind the pike in a food processor, or use a tamis if you are lucky enough to have one. Set aside.

Bring the water to a boil. Sift in the flour and stir until the water is absorbed. Keep stirring so that the mixture doesn't stick to the pan. Remove from the heat and beat in one of the eggs. Cool the mixture, then refrigerate until cold.

Remove the mixture from the refrigerator and blend it in a food processor until smooth. This mixture is called a *panade* in French cooking.

Cream the butter in a small bowl. Put the ground pike in a bowl that is set inside another bowl of ice. Season with salt and pepper, mix in the panade, and gradually add the other whole egg and the egg yolks. When blended well, add the butter. This can be done in a food processor if all ingredients are kept cold. Chill the mixture for 30 minutes.

To make the white sauce, place the chicken stock in a heavy saucepan over medium heat. Bring to a simmer, then reduce the heat and continue to simmer on low until the stock is reduced down to 1 cup liquid, about 45 minutes. This makes a very concentrated stock.

In a large saucepan over medium heat,

continued on next page

reduce the cream until it begins to thicken, whisking occasionally.

Whisk the thickened cream into the stock, adding more or less cream, depending on the desired consistency. Season with salt and pepper to taste. Strain the sauce through a fine-mesh sieve, if desired. Makes 2 cups.

To assemble the dish, shape the quenelles by mounding the mixture between 2 warmed spoons. Set each quenelle on a floured surface.

Preheat the oven to 400 degrees Fahrenheit. Butter a baking dish large enough to hold the quenelles. In a wide saucepan, bring 3 quarts of water to a boil and poach the quenelles for 15 minutes without letting the water boil. Drain thoroughly. Arrange the quenelles in the prepared baking dish.

Nap the quenelles with enough white sauce to cover. Sprinkle with the Parmesan cheese. Bake for 15 to 20 minutes, until the cheese browns. Serve 2 to 3 quenelles per diner.

Makes 6 servings.

Braised Meat Roast

To adapt this recipe for moose or caribou, baste frequently and cook to an internal temperature of 120 degrees Fahrenheit to avoid drying out the lean game meat.

6-inch-thick chuck roast of beef (about 5 pounds)

8 cloves garlic, peeled and cut in half

2 bacon strips, cut into ½-inch pieces

Salt and freshly ground pepper to taste

2 tablespoons unsalted butter

1 cup diced carrots

1 cup diced celery

1 cup diced onion

2 cups red wine

3 to 4 cups homemade or canned beef stock

2 sprigs fresh oregano, or 1 teaspoon dried

1 tablespoon juniper berries or 3 ounces of gin

1 teaspoon ground anise

2 tablespoons all-purpose flour

Preheat the oven to 375 degrees Fahrenheit. Cut slits in the meat with a small, sharp knife. Insert the garlic and bacon into the slits. Sprinkle the meat with salt and pepper to taste. In a large metal roasting pan, heat the butter and brown the roast on both sides over medium heat. Add the carrots, celery, and onion, and cook for 10 minutes.

Add the red wine and stir to deglaze, scraping up the bits of solids in the pan. Add the stock, oregano, juniper berries, and anise. Cover the pan and braise in the oven for 2 hours, or until a meat thermometer reads between 120 and 135 degrees Fahrenheit, depending on desired doneness. Remove the roast from the oven and let stand for 15 minutes. Remove any fat from the pan. Thicken the remaining pan juices with the flour, adding water if needed for the desired consistency. Serve immediately.

Makes 8 servings.

Robert Litti's Sauerbraten

It was quite an event when "guest chef" Litti prepared dinner for the lodge. The pleased glow on his face as he served his creation was worth the extra mess in the kitchen! This recipe takes several days to prepare. Serve it with spaetzle (see recipe on page 241).

2 cups water
1 cup wine vinegar
1 teaspoon salt
2 onions, peeled and
*   coarsely chopped*
1 carrot, coarsely chopped
5 peppercorns
2 whole cloves
1 bay leaf
2 juniper berries
2 pounds beef bottom round
5 tablespoons canola oil
Salt and freshly ground
*   pepper to taste*
1 cup crushed gingersnaps
1 cup sour cream
Robert Litti's Spaetzle
*   (see page 241)*

Put the water, vinegar, salt, onion, carrot, peppercorns, cloves, bay leaf, and juniper berries in a large saucepan. Bring to a boil, then reduce the heat and simmer for 15 minutes. Set aside to cool.

Place the meat in an enameled pot. Pour the marinade over the meat, cover loosely, and refrigerate for 2 to 3 days, turning the meat occasionally.

Preheat the oven to 350 degrees Fahrenheit. Drain the meat, reserving the marinade, pat the meat dry with paper towels, and brown it in the oil. Place the meat in a casserole. Strain the marinade, discarding the vegetables, and pour it over the meat. Cook the beef in the oven for 1½ hours, or until a meat thermometer registers 135 degrees Fahrenheit. Remove to a serving platter.

Skim the fat from the sauce and season with salt and pepper to taste. Add the gingersnaps and cook over medium heat until the sauce has thickened. Mix in the sour cream. Slice the sauerbraten and serve it in its sauce with the spaetzle.

Makes 4 servings.

Broiled Lamb Chops with Feta Cheese and Roasted Garlic

The roasted garlic can be made a day ahead of time. The garlic is also great served with Gorgonzola cheese on toast points with a hearty red wine.

3 large whole garlic bulbs
¼ cup olive oil
1 cup crumbled feta cheese
2 cups sliced spinach leaves
2 shallots, peeled and
  minced
2 tablespoons unsalted
  butter
1 cup fine sourdough bread
  crumbs
1 egg
½ teaspoon dried oregano
8 lamb chops (1 to 1½
  inches thick)

Preheat the oven to 350 degrees Fahrenheit. Roast the garlic by cutting off the tops of the cloves and loosening the sides. Place the garlic in foil, pour a little olive oil over the top, and cover with additional foil. Bake for 50 minutes, until the garlic is soft.

Mash the garlic in a bowl. Add the feta cheese. Sauté the spinach and shallots in the butter until the spinach is wilted, and add to the bowl. Add the bread crumbs, egg, and oregano. You may have to add a little stock or water to be able to form the mixture into a ball.

Heat the broiler. Make a 1½-inch cut in the loin side of a lamb chop, down to the center bone, to make a small pocket. Fill with some of the garlic mixture. Repeat with the remaining lamb chops. Broil for 10 to 15 minutes, turning once. Serve immediately.

Makes 4 servings.

Rolled Flank Steak

This dish was prepared on the spur of the moment for a group of us during the flood of 1985 by a Riversong chef of Italian heritage. We were working hard to save our greenhouse as the river threatened to rise over the bank. Flank steak prepared in this way makes an easy and very aromatic dish.

1 cup finely minced celery
1 cup diced onion
4 cloves garlic, peeled and minced
6 tablespoons olive oil
½ cup shredded Parmesan cheese
2 eggs
3 cups torn fresh sourdough bread
5 cups homemade or canned beef stock
1 flank steak, 3 to 4 pounds
1 cup sliced onion
3 cloves garlic, peeled and sliced
1 cup red wine
1 cup crushed tomatoes

Preheat the oven to 350 degrees Fahrenheit. In a wide sauté pan over medium heat, sauté the celery, onion, and garlic in 3 tablespoons of the olive oil until soft. Place the mixture in a medium bowl. Add the cheese, eggs, bread, and 1 cup of the stock. Mix well.

Butterfly the flank steak by slicing it in half horizontally, cutting it almost through so that when opened it resembles butterfly wings. Lightly pound the meat flat. Cover the steak with the bread mixture, roll it up, and tie with butcher's string. Place a roasting pan on top of the stove with the remaining 3 tablespoons olive oil and heat over medium-high heat. Brown the steak on all sides. Add the onion and garlic. Cook on the stovetop for 10 minutes. Add the wine and stir to deglaze, scraping the pan. Add the tomato and the remaining stock. Braise the meat for 1 hour on the center rack of the oven. Remove from the oven and let stand for 15 minutes. Slice the meat and serve with the pan juices.

Makes 6 to 8 servings.

Anne Willan's Quick Brioche Dough

This dough is versatile. Incredibly rich, it can be used to make bread for sandwiches or to make a breakfast bread or even a dessert.

*1 tablespoon (1 package)
    active dry yeast*
¼ teaspoon sugar
*¼ cup warm water (110 to
    115 degrees Fahrenheit)*
*2 cups sifted all-purpose
    flour*
1 teaspoon salt
2 tablespoons sugar
6 eggs, beaten
*1 cup unsalted butter, cut
    into pieces and softened*

Dissolve the yeast and ¼ teaspoon sugar in the warm water. Let stand until foamy, 5 to 10 minutes. Sift the flour, salt, and two tablespoons of the sugar onto a clean, smooth surface.

Make a well in the center of the flour and add the yeast mixture with the beaten eggs. Work with your hands to make a smooth dough. Knead the dough on a floured board, lifting it up and throwing it down until it is very elastic. Work in more flour if necessary. Transfer the dough to an oiled bowl and let rise in a warm place for 1 to 1½ hours, or until doubled in bulk. Knead lightly to knock out the air, and work in the softened butter. Anne Willan recommends smearing the dough across the table surface to mix all the ingredients well.

To bake the bread, preheat the oven to 425 degrees Fahrenheit. Shape the dough into loaves or rolls. Let rise until almost doubled in bulk, 20 to 30 minutes. Bake at 425 degrees Fahrenheit for 15 minutes, then reduce the heat to 375 degrees Fahrenheit and continue baking for 20 to 30 minutes, until the loaf is golden and the bottom of the bread is crusty.

Makes 2 large loaves.

Anne Willan's Salmon in Brioche Crust

Anne used this recipe when she conducted her culinary weekend at the lodge.

1 recipe Anne Willan's Quick Brioche Dough (see recipe on page 249)
1 salmon (4 to 5 pounds), scaled and cleaned, with head on
1 to 2 tablespoons canola oil, for brushing
1 egg, beaten with ½ teaspoon salt, for glaze
Salt and freshly ground pepper to taste
Fresh herbs, such as thyme, basil, and parsley

Make the brioche dough and let it rise in a warm place. Wash the fish and dry thoroughly, inside and out, with paper towels. Cut off the fins and trim the tail to a **V**.

Divide the brioche dough in half and roll out one half to the length of the fish. Place on a well-buttered baking sheet, brush with oil, set the fish on top, lying on its side, and trim the dough, leaving a 1-inch border around the edge of the fish. Brush the border of the dough with egg glaze. Add the dough trimmings to the remaining dough and roll it out to the length of the fish. Season the fish, inside and out, with salt and pepper, brush it with oil, set a bunch of herbs inside the cavity, and cover the fish with the dough. Press the edges of the dough together to seal them, trim the excess, and push the ends in to neaten. Brush the dough with the egg glaze

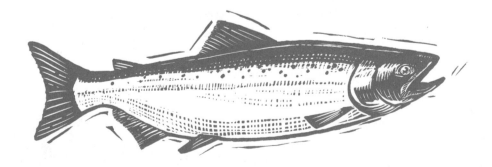

and decorate it, using scissors to make scales and mark the tail in lines. The fish, tightly covered with plastic wrap, can be kept overnight in the refrigerator, or it can be frozen.

To bake the fish, preheat the oven to 425 degrees Fahrenheit. Let the brioche rise in a warm place for 30 to 45 minutes, or until slightly puffed. Bake for 10 minutes, then reduce the heat to 375 degrees Fahrenheit and bake 30 to 35 minutes more. Transfer the fish to a large platter. At the table, cut around the edge of the fish to loosen the top crust, and lift it off to expose the fish. Carve the fish from the bone as usual, and serve a piece of brioche with each portion.

Makes 8 to 10 servings.

Maggie Hayes's Riversong Lodge Oatmeal Cookies

Maggie is an ear surgeon from the hospital where Carl and I used to work. She comes out each summer and helps with cookie duty. These are old-fashioned oatmeal cookies with just a hint of orange and the modern addition of chocolate chips.

2 cups all-purpose flour
1 teaspoon baking soda
1 teaspoon salt
1 cup unsalted butter or
 margarine
1 cup granulated sugar
1 cup light brown sugar,
 packed
2 eggs
2 tablespoons orange juice
1 tablespoon plus 1 teaspoon
 grated orange peel
2 cups quick-cooking rolled
 oats
1 cup chopped walnuts
1 cup miniature chocolate
 chips

Preheat the oven to 375 degrees Fahrenheit. Sift the flour with the baking soda and salt. Cream the butter in a large mixing bowl and gradually add the sugars, creaming until light and fluffy. Add the eggs, orange juice, and orange peel, mixing well. Blend together the flour and butter mixtures. Add the oats, blending well but not overmixing. Stir in the walnuts and the chocolate chips. Drop by level tablespoonfuls onto an ungreased cookie sheet about 2 inches apart. Bake for 12 to 15 minutes, or until golden.

Makes 60 cookies.

Conversion Charts

Alaska Source List

Other Books on Alaskan Cooking

Index

Conversion Charts

Liquid Measures

Fluid Ounces	U.S. Measurements	Imperial Measurements	Milliliters
¼	2 teaspoons	1 dessert spoon	7
½	1 tablespoon	1 tablespoon	15
1	2 tablespoons	2 tablespoons	30
2	¼ cup	4 tablespoons	59
4	½ cup		118
6	¾ cup		177
8	1 cup (½ pint)		236
10	1¼ cups		295
12	1½ cups		355
16	2 cups (1 pint)		473
18	2¼ cups		532 (½ liter)
20	2½ cups	1 pint	591
24	3 cups		710
28	3½ cups		798
32	4 cups (2 pints, 1 quart)		946
36	4½ cups		1065 (1 liter)

Solid Measures

U.S. Ounces	Pounds	Metric Grams	Kilos
1		28	
2		57	
4	¼	113	
6		170	
8	½	227	
12	¾	340	
16	1	454	
20	1¼	567	
28	1¾	794	
32	2	907	
36	2¼	1021	1 (approximate)

Oven Temperatures

°Fahrenheit	Gas Mark	°Celsius	Heat of Oven
250	½	121	Very low
300	2	148	Low
325–350	3–4	163–177	Moderate
375–400	5–6	190–204	Fairly hot
425	7	218	Hot
450	8	232	Very hot

Alaska Source List

SOURCES OF INFORMATION
Riversong Lodge:
  Carl and Kirsten Dixon
  Riversong Lodge
  2463 Cottonwood Street
  Anchorage, AK 99508
  907-274-2710
  Fax 907-277-6256

Alaska travel:
  State of Alaska Division of Tourism
  P.O. Box 110801
  Juneau, AK 99811-0801
  907-465-2010

Alaska seafoods:
  Alaska Seafood Marketing Institute
  1111 West 8th Street, Suite 100
  Juneau, AK 99801-1895
  907-586-2902

MAIL-ORDER SOURCES FOR ALASKAN PRODUCTS
Alaska honey:
  Southcentral Alaska Beekeepers Association
  P.O. Box 141976
  Anchorage, AK 99504

  Alaska Honey and Pollen Company
  15524 Old Glenn Highway
  Eagle River, AK 99577

Alaska game meats, reindeer, and reindeer sausage (officially called "Alaska sausage with reindeer meat"):
    Alaska Sausage & Seafood
    2914 Arctic Boulevard
    Anchorage, AK 99503

    Indian Valley Meats
    HC 52 8809 Huot Circle
    Bird Indian, AK 99540

    Trappers Creek
    5650 B Street
    Anchorage, AK 99502

Alaska seafoods and smoked seafoods:
    Alaska Sausage & Seafood
    2914 Arctic Boulevard
    Anchorage, AK 99503

    Trappers Creek
    5650 B Street
    Anchorage, AK 99502

Alaska wild berry jams, jellies, syrups, and candies:
    Alaska Wild Berry Products
    800 East Dimond Boulevard
    Anchorage, AK 99515

    Alaska Wilderness Gourmet, Inc.
    219 East International Airport Road
    Anchorage, AK 99518

Other Books on Alaskan Cooking

Alaska Cook Book. Seward, Alaska: Seward Gateway Publishing Company, n.d.

Alaska Farm Structures, Inc. *From Alaska's Country Kitchens.* Alaska Farm Structures, 1982.

ALASKA magazine editors. *Alaska Wild Berry Guide and Cookbook.* Seattle: Alaska Northwest Books, 1982.

Alaska Seafood Marketing Institute. *Alaska's Seafood Cookbook.* Juneau: The Alaska Seafood Marketing Institute, 1987.

The Alaskan Camp Cook. Seattle: Alaska Northwest Books, 1973.

Alaskan Dog Mushers. *Trail Food and Old Fashioned Recipe Book, with Old Fashioned Remedies Throughout.* Wasilla, Alaska: L & B Color Printing, 1989.

Alaskan Scottish Club. *The Alaskan Scottish Cookbook.* 4th ed. Shawnee Mission, Kansas: Circulation Service, 1984.

Aldrin, Beverly, ed. *Alaskan Sourdough and Wild Game Cookbook.* Anchorage: Arctic Circle Enterprises, 1981.

Alexandra. *Eskimo Cookbook.* Saanichton, B.C.: Hancock House, 1977.

Allman, Ruth. *Alaska Sourdough.* Seattle: Alaska Northwest Books, 1976.

Anchorage Women's Club. *Alaska's Cooking.* Anchorage: Anchorage Women's Club, 1959.

Anchorage Women's Club. *Alaska's Cooking.* 2d rev. ed. Anchorage: The Anchorage Women's Club, 1976.

Babcock, Pat, and Diane Shaw. *Cooking in Alaska: The Land of the Midnight Sun.* Norfolk, Virginia: Donning Co., 1988.

Bear Paw Committee. *Bear Paw Cookbook.* Eagle River, Alaska: Bear Paw Committee, 1987.

Binford, Lewis Roberts. *Nunamiut Ethnoarchaeology.* New York: Academic Press, 1978.

Brock, Susan, John and Nancy Decherney, and Deborah Marshall. *The Fiddlehead Cookbook: Recipes from Alaska's Most Celebrated Restaurant and Bakery.* New York: St. Martin's Press, 1991.

Brown, Dale. *American Cooking: The Northwest.* New York: Time-Life Books, 1970.

Brunner, Fr. Bill. *The Greater Yukon Cookbook, Galena, Alaska.* Waterloo, Iowa: G & R Publishing Co., 1978.

Business and Professional Women's Club. *Alaska's Capital City Cook Book.* Juneau: Business and Professional Women's Club, 1962.

Carey, Mary Latch. *Let's Taste Alaska.* Willow, Alaska: Tex-Alaska Manuscripts, 1982.

Cleveland, Bess Anderson. *Alaskan Cookbook.* 2d ed. Berkeley, Calif.: Howell-North, 1970.

Coats, Leah. *Alaskan Fish Book.* Sitka, Alaska: Old Harbor Books, 1981.

Cogo, Nora and Robert. *Haida Food from Land and Sea.* Anchorage: Materials Development Center Rural Education, University of Alaska, n.d.

Cole, Jerryne. *A Cache of Recipes from Camp Denali.* Camp Denali: Denali National Park and Preserve, Alaska, 1979.

Business and Professional Women's Club. *Cook Book, Featuring Recipes of Alaskan Products.* Juneau: Business and Professional Women's Club, 1935.

Cooking Alaskan. Seattle: Alaska Northwest Books, 1983.

Dirks, Moses. *Nii^gu^gim Qalgadangis = Atkan Food.* Anchorage: National Bilingual Materials Development Center, Rural Education, 1980.

Easter Seal Society. *Out of Alaska's Kitchens.* Rev. ed. Anchorage: Easter Seal Society for Alaska Crippled Children and Adults, 1961.

The Federation. *Potlatch Cookbook.* Anchorage: Van Cleve Printing Inc., 1980.

Fisher, Phyllis, ed. *The Alaskan Wild Game Cookbook.* Anchorage: Color Art Printing Company, 1961.

Gerken, Mary, and Cass Crandall. *Alaska Cooking Classics, A Treasury of Lodge and Bed and Breakfast Favorite Recipes.* Homer, Alaska: Kachemak Publishing, 1991.

Heaven Scent, An Alaskan Jewish Cookbook. Lexena, Kansas: Cookbook Publishers, 1980.

Hunter, Alice. *Alice Hunter's North Country Cookbook.* Yellowknife, Northwest Terr.: Northern Publishers, 1986.

Jones, Anore. *Nauriat Niginaqtuat, Plants that we Eat.* Kotzebue, Alaska: Traditional Nutrition Project, Maniilaq Association, 1983.

Juneau Seniors in Action. *A Gourmet Guide to Seal Flippers and Salmonberries: A Collection of Food Gathering Traditions and Recipes from Southeast Alaskan Grandparents.* Juneau: Juneau Seniors in Action, 1987.

Kalugin, Marina, Elena Martushev, and Julie Yakunin. *Russian Old Believer Cookbook.* Nilolaevsk, Alaska: Nilolaevsk School, 1984.

Kashevaroff, Sasha, trans. *Famous Russian Recipes.* 3d ed. Sitka, Alaska: Old Harbor Press, 1985 (1st ed., 1936).

Kenai Peninsula Historical Association. *Kenai Peninsula's Favorite Recipes.* Kenai, Alaska: Kenai Peninsula Historical Association, 1988.

Kodiak Fishermen's Wives. *More Memoirs of a Galley Slave.* Kodiak, Alaska: Kodiak Fishermen's Wives, Non-Profit Inc., n.d.

Lesh, Sally. *A Collection of Recipes from Gustavus Inn.* Gustavus, Alaska: Gustavus Inn, 1973.

Mills, Mrs. H. A. *Student Loan Fund Cookbook: A Collection of Reliable Formulas which Have Been Tested and Found To Be of the Best.* Anchorage: Press of *Anchorage Times* Publishing Co., 1926.

Morris, Nanci A. *Just for the Halibut: Alaskan Halibut Recipes.* Anchorage: Flatfish Publishing, 1988.

NCO Wives. *Eating in the Land of the Midnight Sun.* Anchorage: Noncommissioned Officers Wives, 1962.

Nelson, Gordon R. *Hibrow Cow: More Alaskan Stories and Recipes.* Seattle: Alaska Northwest Books, 1989.

Nelson, Gordon R. *Lowbush Moose (and Other Alaskan Recipes).* Seattle: Alaska Northwest Books, 1978.

Nelson, Gordon R. *Smokehouse Bear: More Alaskan Recipes and Stories.* Seattle: Alaska Northwest Books, 1982.

Nibeck, Cecilia. *Alaskan Halibut Recipes.* Anchorage: Alaska Enterprises, 1989.

Owsichek, Lorane. *Lorane Owsichek's Moose Stew and Caviar from Fishing Unlimited.* Anchorage: Fishing Unlimited, n.d.

Page, Winni. *Panning for Pleasure: A Juneau, Alaska, Cookbook.* Memphis, Tenn: S. C. Toof and Company, 1988.

Peter, Mary Scott. *One Hundred Years in the Kitchen.* Pipestone, Minn.: Nicollet Press, 1980.

Pioneers of Alaska Auxiliary No. 4. *Pioneers of Alaska Cookbook.* Olathe, Kansas: Cookbook Publishers, 1988.

Self, Ronald A. *Alaska Trappers Cookin' Book.* Sitka, Alaska: Woodsmoke Outfitters, 1985.

Shaw, Diane, ed. *Bake Off Cookbook, Tanana Valley Fair.* Fairbanks: Tanana Valley Fair Committee, 1981.

Shelby, Jerome. *The Alaskan Musher's Cookbook.* Fairbanks: InfoSystems, 1983.

Stewart, Jane, and Betty Harris. *Juneau Centennial Cookbook.* Juneau: Juneau Centennial Committee, 1983.

A Taste of Alaska: Great Recipes from the Top of the World. Anchorage: Polar Bay Products, 1989.

The Two Billion Dollar Cookbook. Anchorage: Ken Wray's Printing Inc., 1990.

White, Helen A. *Alaska Wildberry Trails (with recipes).* Rev. ed. Anchorage: University of Alaska Extension Bulletin, 1959.

Women of the Moose Chapter No. 139. *Favorite Recipes.* Kansas City, Missouri: Bev-Ron Publishing Co., 1960.

Index

pie, 132; salmon, smoked, noodles, 161; salmon, smoked, pizza, 42; salmon, steamed in paper, 163; soy-sesame marinade for, 156; stock, Asian, 164. *See also* crab; scallops; shrimp

flank steak, rolled, 248

flowers, edible, 148

French toast, honey nut, 100

Fresh Beet Relish, 205

Fresh Egg Pasta, 129

Frikadeller Soup, 113

fritters, seafood and brown rice, with herbs, 190

fruit leather, 191

galette, smoked duck and potato, 214

game, honey-pepper marinade for, 118. *See also* caribou; moose; rabbit; reindeer

game birds, horseradish ginger crust for, 188. *See also* grouse

garlic: and potatoes, sautéed, 230; roasted, 247; roasted, with lamb chops and feta cheese, 247

ginger and sorrel jelly, 204

Glazed Corned Beef with Orange Horseradish Sauce, 105

goose, roasted, 43

Green and Red Tomato Relish, 199

Green Bean Salad with Soy-Sesame Dressing, 156

green bean(s): and broccoli patties, 142; salad with soy-sesame dressing, 156

Green Cabbage Salad, 60

Grilled Red Snapper with Fennel and Cream, 173

grouse, pan-roasted with lemon and herbs, 104

Gruyère cheese and cabbage loaf, 32

halibut: in Alaska Cobb salad, 128; chowder, 87; in paella, 187; pasta with Swiss chard, rhubarb, bacon, and, 114; and brown rice fritters with herbs, 190; with sake kasu, 162

Halibut with Sake Kasu, 162

ham, crusty baked, 89

hash: lamb, 91; vegetable, 232

Hearty Halibut Chowder, 87

Herb Garden Vinaigrette, 145

Homemade Korean Kim Chee, 165

Homemade Marshmallows, 119

honey, 118; apple rolls, 121; frosting glasses with, 118; marinade for fish, 152; nut brittle, 118; nut French toast, 100; orange cheesecake with walnut crust, 117; Pennies from Heaven, 45; pepper marinade, 118; substituting for sugar, 118

Honey Apple Rolls, 121

"Honey Love," 118

Honey Marinade for Fish, 152

Honey Nut French Toast, 100

Honey Orange Cheesecake with Walnut Crust, 117

horseradish ginger crust, for fish, chicken, and game birds, 188

Hot Danish Potato Salad, 183

"How to Clean a Fish," 159-60

Japanese Eggplant Ratatouille, 158

jar, pumpkin cake in a, 217

jelly: crab apple, 201; mixed berry, 208; sorrel ginger, 204

Jesse's Cabbage Salad, 231

juniper berries, carrots and onions with honey and, 149

About the Author

Through Kirsten Dixon's culinary acclaim, the Riversong Lodge has been written about more than any other Alaskan fishing lodge—most recently by *Men's Journal, New York* magazine, and *Country America* magazine. Kirsten is a food columnist for the *Anchorage Daily News* and a former food writer for *ALASKA* magazine. She has studied at the Cordon Bleu in Paris and with Jacques Pépin at Boston University, and was recently a guest chef at the James Beard House in New York.

Active in the culinary community, Kirsten is a member of the American Culinary Federation, the International Association of Culinary Professionals, and the American Institute of Wine and Food. She is particularly interested in regional foods of Alaska.

A Master Gardener, Kirsten teaches gardening classes in Anchorage during the winter. The lodge greenhouse and expansive garden provide fresh herbs, vegetables, and fruit for Riversong guests.

Kirsten and her husband, Carl, live at Riversong year-round, where they home-school their two young daughters, Carly and Amanda. Their busy lives include two dogs, three cats, chickens, rabbits, geese, ducks, and two pigs.

U.S.News
& WORLD REPORT

2020 EDITION

Best Hospitals

EXCLUSIVE RANKINGS

▶ Get **Expert Care**
in Cancer,
Cardiology,
Neurology,
Orthopedics
and More

▶ The Best
Children's Hospitals
in 10 Specialties

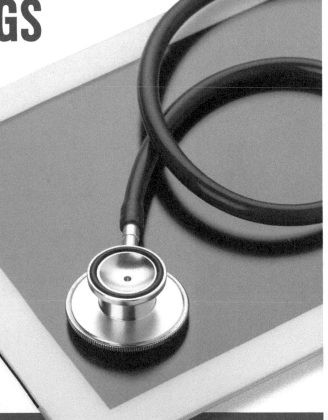

Plus: The Top Hospitals in **Your State**

"I'm an expert at finding you, ~~cancer~~"

Dr. Lavinia Middleton | Cancer Physician

Giving patients an accurate diagnosis means giving them the right treatment plan and the best hope of beating cancer, from the start. At MD Anderson Cancer Center, our world-renowned pathologists correct a new patient's initial diagnosis from another hospital up to 25 percent of the time. **Choose MD Anderson first. Call 1-855-894-0145 or visit MakingCancerHistory.com.**

Ranked number one in the nation for cancer care by U.S. News & World Report.

THE UNIVERSITY OF TEXAS

MD Anderson
~~Cancer~~ Center

Making Cancer History®